MENTORING LEADERS

PART FIVE OF THE DEVELOPING GIFTS AND SKILLS SERIES

DR. HENDRIK J VORSTER

.

CONTENTS

MENTORING LEADERS

PART FIVE OF THE DEVELOPING GIFTS AND SKILLS SERIES

-- Disciple Manual --

Mentoring Leaders
Part Five of the Developing Gifts and Skills Series
(Disciple Manual)
By Dr. Hendrik J. Vorster

For more copies and information please visit and write to us at: www.
churchplantinginstitute.com
resources@churchplantinginstitute.com

ISBN 978-1-955923-17-0

PART I

MENTORING LEADERS

Part Five of the Developing Gifts and Skills Series

1

INTRODUCTION

SESSION ONE

Once you've led two or more people to Christ, you need to gather them for _____, like Jesus did with His Disciples. By teaching our disciples the teachings of Jesus, we in effect _____ them. The most time-efficient way to disciple new Believers is in a _____.

> Acts 20:28 (NIV) *"Keep watch over yourselves and all the flock of which **the Holy Spirit has made you overseers.** Be shepherds of the church of God, which he bought with his own blood."*

As this Scripture highlights, being a shepherd, or overseer of the flock of God, is an honourable appointment of the _____. It is both a huge responsibility and an honour to be entrusted with the welfare of the lives of the children of God.

This weekend encounter will teach us the *how-to* care for our disciples and equip us with skills that will help us to do so with excellence.

Together, we will explore the following areas:

Session One: The Biblical Shepherd

What does the Biblical Shepherd look like? What is the Lord's desire for Shepherds?

Session Two: The heart of a Shepherd

We will look at How we can have a Shepherd's heart. We will look at the Biblical characteristics of a good Shepherd.

Session Three: The purpose of a Shepherd

In this session we will explore what God wants us to do with and for His Sheep.

Session Four: Developing deep and meaningful relationships

This session marks the beginning of a few practical sessions on the "How-to" of building life-long and purposeful relationships.

Session Five: Practical Keys

This session outlines practical and helpful steps to take to lead well, and to provide an atmosphere where people's lives can be transformed by the Power of God.

Session Six: Practical application

This session concludes extremely helpful guidelines on the processes at play in bringing people from various backgrounds together, to ultimately serve together to reach the lost for God.

Session Seven: Consecration Session

During this final session, we conclude, not just this weekend's equipping, but also the entire equipping series of Step Three - Developing Gifts and skills. It would seem appropriate that we take time to present ourselves before God as equipped workers to be sent out to go and to preach the gospel, to make disciples by teaching them and to care for them like Jesus would.

I pray that this Weekend will bring conclusion in your heart as to How you will serve the Father and the expansion of His Kingdom. I pray that it will serve as a huge blessing to you.

2

THE BIBLICAL SHEPHERD
SESSION TWO

T his weekend is all about learning to be a _____.
I am most certain that most of you have at this point of your
journey started sharing your faith, with positive outcomes.
This weekend we will answer the question that many of you
might have:

> *"Now that I have led someone to the Lord, what do I do with them?"*

During this weekend we will explore how to Shepherd those
entrusted to our care. We will learn how to take care of the sheep
entrusted to our care. Shepherds usually take care of their sheep in a
flock. We will learn how to bring the flock together and how to help
them become a fully functioning part of the Body of Christ.

In the Acts of the Apostles we read a clear instruction to Shepherds, which we will attempt to address in a responsible manner
throughout this weekend course.

> *Acts 20:28 (NIV) "Keep watch over yourselves and all the flock of
> which the Holy Spirit has made you overseers. Be shepherds of
> the church of God, which he bought with his own blood."*

We are offered such an amazing privilege to be entrusted with the care of those whom we have the privilege to lead to Christ. Over the following hours together, we will learn all about being a good Shepherd.

Let us start by looking at Shepherds in the Bible.

Abel was the first shepherd we read about in the Bible. The Bible says that: "**Abel kept flocks.**" He was taking care of his flocks.

> *Genesis 4:2 Later she gave birth to his brother Abel. Now **Abel kept flocks**, and Cain worked the soil.*

Rachel is the second Shepherd we read about in the Bible; as she was tending the sheep of her father.

> *Genesis 29:9 While he was still talking with them, **Rachel came with her father's sheep, for she was a shepherd**.*

Through Jacob's marriage to Rachel, He also became a shepherd who tended the sheep of his Father-in-law, at first, but later overseeing a huge livestock of several thousand.

> *Genesis 30:29-30 Jacob said to him, "You know how **I have worked for you and how your livestock has fared under my care**. The little you had before I came has increased greatly, and the Lord has blessed you wherever I have been. But now, when may I do something for my own household?"*

When Jacob was old, before giving up his spirit, he blessed Joseph, and here we see him referencing our Heavenly Father as His Shepherd. He learnt about God as being his Shepherd.

> *Genesis 48:15-16 Then he blessed Joseph and said, "May the God before whom my fathers Abraham and Isaac walked faithfully,*

the God who has been my shepherd all my life to this day, the Angel who has delivered me from all harm —may he bless these boys. May they be called by my name and the names of my fathers Abraham and Isaac, and may they increase greatly on the earth."

Moses was tending his Father-in-law's sheep when God called him to be His Servant to deliver Israel.

*Exodus 3:1 Now **Moses was tending the flock of Jethro his father-in-law**, the priest of Midian, and he led the flock to the far side of the wilderness and came to Horeb, the mountain of God.*

David was tending his Father's sheep when God called and anointed him to be the next King of Israel.

*1 Samuel 16:11 So he asked Jesse, "Are these all the sons you have?" "There is still the youngest," Jesse answered. **"He is tending the sheep."** Samuel said, "Send for him; we will not sit down until he arrives."*

David learnt to care for the sheep of his Father before the Lord used him to become the shepherd of His people, Israel. The Bible teaches that he cared for them with integrity of heart, and with great skill.

*Psalms 78:70-72 **He chose David his servant and took him from the sheep pens; from tending the sheep he brought him to be the shepherd of his people Jacob,** of Israel his inheritance. And **David shepherded them with integrity of heart; with skillful hands he led them.***

Amos was a shepherd before God called and anointed him to be a prophet to His people.

*Amos 7:15 But **the Lord took me from tending the flock** and said to me, 'Go, prophesy to my people Israel.'*

In his great Psalm, David present us with the true heart of a Shepherd.

*Psalm 23:1-6 The Lord is my shepherd, **I lack nothing**. He makes me lie down in green pastures, **he leads me** beside quiet waters, **he refreshes** my soul. **He guides me** along the right paths for his name's sake. Even though I walk through the darkest valley, I will fear no evil, for **you are with me**; your rod and your staff, they **comfort me**. **You prepare a table before me** in the presence of my enemies. **You anoint my head with oil**; my cup overflows. Surely your goodness and love will follow me all the days of my life, and I will dwell in the house of the Lord forever.*

David presents the Good Shepherd as a Provider, a Guide, a Protector, an Anointer, and an ever-present Presence through every circumstance of life.

Jesus presents Himself to us as the Good Shepherd.

*John 10:11 "**I am the good shepherd**. The good shepherd lays down his life for the sheep."*

Many times, and through many of the Prophets, God spoke about raising up "*a Shepherd*" to save His people, to rescue them, and to take proper care of them. One of the most outstanding portions of Scripture, addressing the Biblical role and expectation of a Shepherd, is found in the Book of Ezekiel. God was looking for a Shepherd who will tend His Sheep with His Heart.

*Ezekiel 34:15-16 "**I myself will tend my sheep** and have them lie down, declares the Sovereign Lord. I will search for the lost and bring back the strays. I will bind up the injured and strengthen*

the weak, but the sleek and the strong I will destroy. I will
shepherd the flock with justice."

Ezekiel 34:31
"You are my sheep, the sheep of my pasture, and I am your God,
declares the Sovereign Lord."'

The Shepherd is that personification of someone who cares, even if it requires to lay down your own life for the sake of the safekeeping of the sheep. The Biblical Shepherd is that person who cares for God's people as if they belonged to them. Very few Shepherds actually care for their own sheep, they normally tend the sheep of others. For the purpose of our time together, God is calling each one of us to walk in the footsteps of Jesus, and to be a Good Shepherd like He is, and wants us to be.

In conclusion on our session on the Biblical Shepherd, let us take a moment to identify the key hallmarks of a biblical shepherd.

Assimilation Application

Group breakout session:

What are the key Hallmarks of a Biblical Shepherd?

Identify Five Good characteristics of a shepherd from Ezekiel 34:1-16.

- 1.
- 2.
- 3.
- 4.
- 5.

Identify Five good characteristics of a good shepherd from John 10:1-18.

- 1.
- 2.
- 3.
- 4.
- 5.

Identify five bad characteristics of bad shepherds from Ezekiel 34:1-16.

- 1.
- 2.
- 3.
- 4.
- 5.

Identify five bad characteristics of bad shepherds from John 10:1-18.

- 1.
- 2.
- 3.
- 4.
- 5.

Which other Scriptures really spoke to you of being a good Shepherd, and what specifically do you aspire to take home with you from that Scripture?

THE HEART OF A SHEPHERD

SESSION THREE

In this session we will look at what the _____ attitude of a Biblical Shepherd looks like. The Word of God teaches us about this heart attitude in a number of Scriptures. Let us look at these for a few moments.

In this session we will look at the heart of a Shepherd, and then also what it is not. Shepherds are those people who take care of the welfare of other believers, by leading them, guiding them, caring and protecting them.

Shepherds have a Self-sacrificing heart

Almost every Shepherd works in the care of someone else. They care for someone else's sheep. The first heart attitude for us to adopt is that of a self-sacrificing _____. We are entrusted with taking care of God's sheep. Christ purchased the sheep that we care for with his own blood.

*Ezekiel 34:31 _____ **are my sheep, the sheep of my** _____,*
and I am your God, declares the Sovereign Lord.'"

*Psalms 100:3 Know that the Lord is God. It is he who made us, and
we are his; we are his people, the sheep of his pasture.*

Revelation chapter 5 present us with "***the Lamb***" who purchased
men from '***every tongue, tribe and nation***' for our God. He became the
Lamb of God to purchase the precious lives of those who would
become sheep of His pasture, under the care of the Great Shepherd.
Jesus became our example of the perfect Shepherd who _____
down His life for the life of the sheep.

*John 10:11 "I am the good shepherd. The good shepherd lays down
his life for the sheep."*

The Shepherd lives for the welfare of the sheep of God. One of
the hallmarks of a Follower of Jesus Christ is that he lays down his
life for the sake of Christ. This is one of the requirements Jesus laid
down for His Followers.

*Luke 9:23 Then he said to them all: "If anyone would come after me,
he must _____ himself and take up his cross daily and
follow me."*

*1 Corinthians 4:15 Even though you have ten thousand guardians in
Christ, **you do not have many fathers,** for **in Christ Jesus I
became your father** through the gospel.*

Every Shepherd lays down his life for the sheep entrusted to his
care. One way of looking at it is like having and caring for your own
children. Who of us, as parents, won't do anything we can for the
welfare of our children? We do whatever it takes to care for our children. Being a Shepherd is like being a spiritual father or mother who
have been entrusted with the care of spiritual children.

To assume responsibility for those whom Jesus paid a high price
for their salvation, requires of us to lay down our lives for the welfare
of the sheep. Being a Shepherd is a selfless, self-sacrificing vocation.

Shepherds have a Willing heart

God is calling on us to be His Shepherds, not because we must, "***But because we are*** _____." Our eagerness to serve is no better expressed than by our willingness to serve the Will of the Father by caring for His Sheep whom He purchased with His blood and sacrifice. One aspect of this is to commit oneself to be an example for others to follow.

> *1 Peter 5:2-4 Be shepherds of God's flock that is under your care, watching over them—not because you must, but **because you are** _____, as God wants you to be; not pursuing dishonest gain, but **eager to serve**; 3 not lording it over those entrusted to you, but **being examples to the flock**. 4 And when the Chief Shepherd appears, you will receive the crown of glory that will never fade away.*

We also see from this Scripture in 1 Peter, the extension of this idea of it being the Will of God to take care of the sheep and to watch over their welfare and well-being. It is God's Will that we take care of His Sheep. God wants and desires us to take care of His Sheep. Our "willingness" to serve the Father, in caring for His Sheep, shows the true heart with which we serve Him. May God find in each one of us a "willingness" to care for His Sheep like He would if He was doing it Himself.

Shepherds have a Caring heart

God is calling us to take _____ of ourselves and over all the flock He placed under our care. To take care requires both to protect and to provide for the sheep what they need most.

There is this saying:

> "*People don't care how much you know until they know how much you* _____."

Once people know that you love them, warts and all, they feel loved and cared for. One other hallmark of Believers is their love for one another.

> John 13:34-35 *"A new command I give you: Love one another. As I have loved you, so you must love one another. 35 By this all men will know that you are my disciples, if you love one another."*

For us as under-shepherds it is to provide _____ from all evil and worldliness, as well as _____ them to green pastures where they will find rest and restoration of their souls. The greatest care we could provide is constantly leading those entrusted to our care, to the Word of God and reliant submissions of prayer. By constantly praying with them and submitting everything through prayer unto God, and exploring and sharing the Word of God together, we actively care for their spiritual wellbeing.

This exhortation is carefully explained in the first letter of Peter, as well as the well-known Psalms 23.

> 1 Peter 5:2-4 **Be shepherds of God's flock that is under your care, watching over them**—*not because you must, but because you are willing, as God wants you to be; not pursuing dishonest gain, but eager to serve; 3 not lording it over those entrusted to you, but being examples to the flock. 4 And when the Chief Shepherd appears, you will receive the crown of glory that will never fade away.*

> Psalms 23:2-3 *He makes me lie down in green pastures, he leads me beside quiet waters, he refreshes my soul. He guides me along the right paths for his name's sake.*

In the words of the Prophet Ezekiel it is extended in greater detail. The Lord spoke through Ezekiel and expressed His dismay that the Shepherds of Israel only took care of themselves and not of the flock over which He assigned them. Shepherds should take care of the flock, and not only for what they may benefit from them.

> *Ezekiel 34:2 "Son of man, prophesy against the shepherds of Israel; prophesy and say to them: 'This is what the Sovereign Lord says:* **Woe to you shepherds of Israel who only take care of yourselves! Should not shepherds take care of the flock?**

The Lord continues throughout this entire chapter to outline what that care looks like.

Caring requires us to:

- *strengthen the _____,*
- *_____ the sick,*
- *_____ up the injured,*
- *search for the _____, and to*
- *Bring back those who have _____ away from God.*

To this end, each one of us, as followers of Jesus Christ, have been called to strengthen the weak, heal the sick, bind up the injured, search for the lost, and to bring back to Him those who have strayed away from their faith in Him.

> *Ezekiel 34:4 You have not strengthened the weak or healed the sick or bound up the injured. You have not brought back the strays or searched for the lost. You have ruled them harshly and brutally.*

Every shepherd is like a parent over their own children. One of the ways we care and protect them is by never exposing the weaknesses of our children to others. When we get close to people, we get close to their weaknesses and failures. Sheep smell. When we get close to our sheep we deal with where they are at with compassion.

Frequently we read about God's concern and care for his people when he refers to them being "*sheep without a shepherd.*" May we care in such a way that the Lord knows that there exists a compassionately caring shepherd in their lives.

Shepherds knows the heart of their sheep

One of the key essentials of being a good shepherd is that you _____ your sheep. It is essential that we know our sheep by _____ and that they know our _____. Know the condition of their lives and that of their family situation.

> John 10:3 *The watchman opens the gate for him, and the sheep listen to his voice.* **He calls his own sheep by name** *and leads them out.*

> John 10:14 *"I am the good shepherd;* **I know my sheep** *and my sheep know me–*

The heart of a shepherd is seen in how he relates with the sheep. How we talk about those entrusted to our care, tells of our intimate knowledge of their wellbeing and condition.

We are Good Shepherds when **we protect them, watch over them** and constantly **watch over their growth, condition and development.** Whenever we observe areas of need or diversions, we address those in a private and caring manner.

Sheep quickly know that you've got their best interest at heart and that you know them better than they know themselves. This intimate knowledge is not for lording it over them or for being busy bodies into their private affairs, but we observe enough, *through prayer and travailing*, that we can help and guide them, and *ultimate care for them effectively.*

We will often find that *the Holy Spirit will* _____ *us to areas of growth and activation* in our disciples lives, but He will also *forewarn us* of encroaching and encumbering situations that might hinder the growth and development in their lives. As Good Shepherds we keep a careful watch over our disciples, as to How we may best care, protect and guide them in their walk with the Lord.

Shepherds are Committed to lead

Shepherds _____ the sheep. Shepherds do not drive the sheep. In Psalm 23 we read about how the Good Shepherd "*leads*" his sheep to green pastures and still waters.

- We lead by our _____.
- We lead by modelling Christ through our behavior, _____ and words.
- We lead by seeing and _____ where they need to go.

True shepherds are those who **constantly look ahead** and know where they are leading towards, and carefully take every precaution to ensure that they lead all the sheep towards that place.

> *Psalms 23:2 2 He makes me lie down in green pastures, he leads me beside quiet waters, 3 he restores my soul. He guides me in paths of righteousness for his name's sake.*

> *John 10:3-4 3 The watchman opens the gate for him, and the sheep listen to his voice. He calls his own sheep by name and leads them out. 4 When he has brought out all his own, he goes on ahead of them, and his sheep follow him because they know his voice.*

Shepherds leads people by going _____ of them. The hireling tells people where they need to go whereas the Shepherd shows the people where he is leading them towards.

The heart with which we lead is observed in the commitment we make to being an example that they can follow.

Assimilation Application

David was known for being a man *"after God's own heart."* I pray that God will find in each one of us, a man or a woman, after His own heart.

> Jeremiah 3:15 (NIV) 15 Then *I will give you shepherds after my own heart*, who will lead you with knowledge and understanding.

> Acts 13:22 (NIV) 22 After removing Saul, he made David their king. God testified concerning him: 'I have found David son of Jesse, *a man after my own heart*; he will do everything I want him to do.'

Let us take a moment and commit ourselves to being good Shepherds. May God find in us people who have a heart after Him, and a heart for His work and for His people. May our actions show the heart we have for Him and for His Sheep. I almost want us to pray the words of David, when He asked God to create in him "a new heart."

> Psalms 51:10 (NIV) 10 Create in me a pure heart, O God, and renew a steadfast spirit within me.

I pray that God will create in us *"a pure heart"* so that we will serve His Sheep with integrity of heart, with sincerity to see the best God has for them accomplished. I pray that God will remove the heart of stone and give us a heart of flesh so that we can serve with love, care, forbearance, understanding, and compassion.

> Ezekiel 11:19 (NIV) 19 *I will give them an undivided heart* and put a new spirit in them; I will remove from them their *heart of stone* and *give them a heart of flesh*.

> Ezekiel 36:26 (NIV) 26 I will give you a new heart and put a

new spirit in you; I will remove from you your heart of stone and give you a heart of flesh.

As an expression of this desire to have a heart after God, let us articulate our commitment to Him in prayer. Take a few moments in quiet prayer and meditation and make these commitments to God (*Give about 10 minutes for this prayerful conclusion of this session*):

- *Lord, I lay down my life for the sheep You entrusted to me, and*
- *I commit to be a willing servant eager to do all that is required of me as an under-shepherd, and*
- *I commit to care for the sheep as if it is You Yourself caring for Your sheep, and*
- *I commit to know the sheep intimately, and*
- *To lead them, by example, to wherever You desire them to go and grow.*
- *Today I declare my eagerness, willingness and desire to strengthen the weak, heal the sick, bind up the wounded, seek the lost and search with eagerness those who have strayed from their faith in You Lord Jesus. Amen!*

May our heart tell of the love we have for God, His work, and His people.

Have a heart for God, His work and His Sheep!

4

THE PURPOSE OF A SHEPHERD
SESSION FOUR

The purpose of a Shepherd is to **care** for the sheep by
_____ and _____ for them.

**"We all have a need and a desire to be _____ and to be
cared for."**

As we've discussed and seen so far, it is both God's desire to care
for His sheep, as well as to Shepherd His sheep through His Servants.
We are His Servants when we avail ourselves to _____ and
_____ for others, on His behalf.

Many times we see young people showing great interest in children. This is wonderful, however, the depth of this love and care for
children is only truly observed when they have their own children,
when the reality of commitment, care and devotion truly come into
play. It is fairly easy to love God's children from afar, especially if you
don't assume responsibility for their well-being, development and
growth. For us, as Shepherds of God's Sheep, **it requires a whole
other level of commitment** and **devotion.**

In this session we will explore **the best ways** in which we can take up our responsibility to care and provide for those entrusted to our care.

The best way to Disciple someone is to step up into the role of being a _____ for them. The greatest expression of making a Disciple is seen in those who shepherd people on Christ's behalf. Our eagerness to serve the Lord is seen by the way in which we seek to save the lost and those who have gone astray, and to then follow through by taking care of them.

Jesus called us to "*go and make disciples of all nations*" and that includes "*baptizing and teaching*" them. The '*teaching*' part is the most comprehensive and engaging part and requires the greatest level of _____ and endurance.

> Matthew 28:19 "*Therefore, go and make disciples of all nations, baptizing them in the name of the Father and of the Son and of the Holy Spirit, 20 and teaching them to obey everything I have commanded you. And surely, I am with you always, to the very end of the age.*"

To be a Shepherd requires skills

To serve as a Shepherd to those God entrusted to our care is a noble call and task and requires _____ beyond our willingness to answering such a call. The skills required are varied, however if we keep at the forefront of our minds who we do this for, and the joy of knowing the eternal impact in the lives of those entrusted to our care, it will move us to apply ourselves with diligence and to continually give our best.

Shepherds provide a caring environment within which they will practice protection and provision.

To develop a _____ environment, we need to develop an "one another," edifying and encouraging, kind of deep relationship between the group members.

1 Thessalonians 5:11 Therefore _____ ***one***
*   **another** and* _____ ***each other up,*** *just as in*
*   fact you are doing.*

How do we encourage and build each other up?

- We _____ one another continually, especially in those areas where we observe growth and development in our faith.
- We speak the _____ in love, even when it requires confrontation.
- We _____ each other on towards love and good deeds.
- We pray for each other and _____ words of encouragement to one another.
- We _____ each other's burdens.
- We love one another by actively _____ felt ways to give expression of our love.

Encouragement takes place when we unconditionally love one another. Edification takes place when people have a deep sense of feeling that they are being heard, understood and then, as a result of this feeling of "***being heard,***" they open up to accept and receive, through words of _____, forgiveness, grace, mercy and clear encouragement for the pathway ahead.

In a later session we will look specifically on how to effectively lead our disciples into edifying and encouraging each other. Suffice to say that we ought to love each other as we love God. Loving in ways that is both intentional and felt is the goal. This is how we are known to be His Disciples – by the way we love one another.

Shepherd not only provide an environment where disciples can edify one another, they also provide a _____ where they can help their disciples to grow.

Shepherds protect and provide for the sheep.

We protect by keeping the sheep together, and by keeping them from wondering away, straying and endangering themselves. We protect them against _____ doctrines, _____ mindsets and destructive relationships and environments.

Shepherds protect their sheep by prayerfully watching over them.

> *1 Peter 5:2 **Be shepherds of God's flock that is under your care, watching over them**—not because you must, but because you are willing, as God wants you to be; not pursuing dishonest gain, but eager to serve;*

The awareness of _____ starts with us keeping watch over our own walk and stand in the Lord continually. One of the men of God who helped the Church understand "watching" is Watchman Nee, a Chinese evangelist. He said;

> *"We must not only be watchful in keeping the time of prayer but also be watchful during the prayer time so that we may really be effective in prayer."*

Definition of Watching

> "Watching is anticipative spiritual awareness or _____ concerning things that are happening around us."

"Alertness" is defined as *"the ability to anticipate right responses to that which is taking place around us."*

This alertness is especially observed through prayer. It is while we pray for, and over, our disciples, that we respond to those things that come to our mind by the Holy Spirit, which then may prompt us to pray more intentionally and thoroughly for things. We respond to the impulse or promptings of the Holy Spirit in prayer.

Jesus modelled watching

On one occasion Jesus modelled this *"watching"* and *"Alertness"* when He told Peter that; *"Satan wanted to sift him, but He prayed for him."*

> Luke 22:31-32 (NIV) 31 "Simon, Simon, *Satan has asked to sift all of you* as wheat. 32 *But I have* _____ *for you, Simon, that your faith may not fail.* And when you have turned back, strengthen your brothers."

Peter's life was spared as a direct result of Jesus' awareness and alertness in prayer as He watched over those entrusted to His care.

The Holy Spirit is amazing. He always helps us and guides us when we keep our disciples in our prayers. He always teaches us and directs us. The more we live in step with the Holy Spirit, the more we will find ourselves alert and aware of things around us, and in the lives of those entrusted to our care. The Holy Spirit will reveal to us things that might happen, good or bad. The Holy Spirit might make us aware of things He is busy working out in our disciple's lives. The more we spend time being aware and spiritually alert, the more we will find ourselves at the crest of the wave in what the Lord is busy doing in and around our lives. This alertness helps us work more efficiently for God.

"Watching" might be more fully defined as,

- Keeping spiritually awake in order to _____.
- To observe closely.
- To be on the _____.

Spiritual alertness is vital to effective shepherding of those entrusted to our care. Such alertness includes our ability to anticipate or comprehend what is taking place around us.

To "**anticipate**" means "**to act in advance as to prevent.**" Watching is _____ shepherding.

How do we watch over our sheep?

- We keep watch when we constantly _____ over those entrusted to our care.
- We keep watch over them when we _____ God to show us His greater purpose for each one of them. As we speak the purpose of God into their lives, we keep watch over them to ensure that they walk and develop in accordance with the purpose God has for each one of them.
- We keep watch when we _____ their lives and prayerfully consider what guidance, teaching, instruction, or help they might need that will help them become more like Christ.

Shepherds protect their sheep by keeping them together.

As Biblical Shepherds we bring and keep our sheep together so that we can better protect them. Jesus spoke about the shepherd going in through the gate to tend his sheep. That speaks of having them together. Jesus modelled this kind of shepherding by discipling his disciples in a _____. The Shepherd has two pieces of equipment with which to shepherd his sheep: *a Rod and a Staff*. The **Rod** was used for _____ them from dangerous animals, as well as for **discipline**, and **the Staff** was used to **keep the straying** sheep together as a flock, as well as **guiding them.**

> *Psalms 23:4 (Amplified) Yes, though I walk through the [deep, sunless] valley of the shadow of death, I will fear or dread no evil, for You are with me; Your rod [to protect] and Your staff [to guide], they comfort me.*

In His rebuke of the Shepherds of Israel, one of the chief concerns was that the Shepherds allowed the sheep to scatter without **keeping them gathered.** As Shepherds we need to remain with our sheep to look after them.

> *Ezekiel 34:11-13 "For this is what the Sovereign Lord says: 'I myself will search for my sheep and look after them. 12 As **a shepherd** _____ after his scattered flock when he is with them, so will **I look after my sheep. I will rescue them** from all the places where they were scattered on a day of clouds and darkness. 13 I will bring them out from the nations and gather them** from the countries, and I will bring them into their own land. I will pasture them on the mountains of Israel, in the ravines and in all the settlements in the land.'"*

We look after our disciples by keeping them in fellowship together. Jesus discipled His Disciples by gathering them and teaching them in a group. In one sense he kept His sheep together to such an extent that at the end of His earthly ministry He declared that He *"**protected them and kept them safe**,"* and that He "_____ **none**" of those given Him.

> *John 17:12 While I was with them, **I protected them and kept them safe** by that name you gave me. **None has been lost** except the one doomed to destruction so that Scripture would be fulfilled.*

How do we keep our Disciples together?

- We bring them _____ regularly for times of ministering to them as a group.
- We stay in contact with our disciples on _____ basis by phoning them, sharing meals together, visiting them, or by meeting for coffee at some cafe.
- We keep our disciples in the forefront of our hearts and minds by _____ for our disciples on a daily basis.

- We meet together as a group so that we can _____ them together.
- When we bring them together, we allow for equally fair times of _____.
- We take time to _____ together.
- We practice the _____ during our time together.

Shepherds protect their sheep by harnessing them with the Truths of God's Word.

We protect them by teaching them the _____ of God's Word in a systematic and structured way. We protect them by ensuring that they feed and live by the Word of God, and not by the sensory impulses of the world. The antidote for false teachings is to form a hedge of protection around our disciples by bringing them _____ doctrine and teaching. Sound doctrine and teaching harnesses our sheep from wolves.

> *2 Timothy 3:14 But as for you, continue in what you have learned and have become convinced of, because you know those from whom you learned it, 15 and how from infancy you have known **the Holy Scriptures, which are able to make you wise** for salvation through faith in Christ Jesus. 16 **All Scripture is God-breathed and is useful for teaching, rebuking, correcting and training in righteousness**, 17 so that the servant of God **may be thoroughly equipped** for every good work.*

A large portion of Titus chapter 2 is devoted on what he needed to teach the flock. He instructs Titus to teach sound doctrine to the old and young men, the woman, the slaves and the children.

> *Titus 2:1 You, however, must teach what is appropriate to _____ doctrine.*

Titus 2:11-14 "*For the grace of God has appeared that offers salvation to all people. It _____ us to say "No" to ungodliness and worldly passions, and to live self-controlled, upright and godly lives in this present age, while we wait for the blessed hope—the appearing of the glory of our great God and Savior, Jesus Christ, who gave himself for us, to redeem us from all wickedness and to purify for himself a people that are his very own, eager to do what is good*"

Titus 2:15 **These, then, are the things you _____ teach.** *Encourage and rebuke with all authority. Do not let anyone despise you.*

We protect our sheep by teaching the truths of God's Word in a systematic and sound way.

How do we teach them?

- We teach them by ensuring that they live on the Word of God on a _____ basis.
- **We teach** them that the Word of God is the **Foundation** and _____ that relates to **every part of our lives.**
- **We teach** them How to _____ the Word of God.
- **We equip** them by _____ the Equipping Model.
- We teach them by helping and providing a _____ **learning experience** by being more facilitating than telling, especially as they mature in their walk with God.

Shepherds provide an example for their disciples to follow.

We provide for our Disciples by providing them with **an _____ to follow.** We provide them a safe learning atmosphere where they can learn the Word of God, appreciate the Voice of the Holy Spirit, and grow in their faith. Nothing prepares us for life like the Word of God.

The greatest legacy anyone can leave is **their example.** Maybe in your life it might be your Mom or your Dad, or your Pastor who is that model or example that you follow. For each Believer we have this instruction to be good examples.

> *Titus 2:7-8 In everything **set them an** _____ by doing what is good. In your teaching show integrity, seriousness and soundness of speech that cannot be condemned, so that those who oppose you may be ashamed because they have nothing bad to say about us.*

> *1 Timothy 4:12 Don't let anyone look down on you because you are young, but **set an** _____ **for the believers** in speech, in conduct, in love, in faith and in purity.*

> *1 Peter 5:2-4 **Be shepherds of God's flock that is under your care, watching over them**—not because you must, but because you are willing, as God wants you to be; not pursuing dishonest gain, but eager to serve; 3 not lording it over those entrusted to you, but **being** _____ **to the flock.** 4 And when the Chief Shepherd appears, you will receive the crown of glory that will never fade away.*

We provide for our Disciples by giving them **a living example** to follow. Jesus called us to follow in His Footsteps. The Apostle Paul became an example to the Believers and urged them to follow his example. We ought to provide our disciples with an example to follow, otherwise we subscribe to the rule of the pharisees who instructed people to comply to rules and regulations which they themselves did not practiced in their own lives. This instruction came right from the top. **Jesus** told His Disciples that **He gave them an example to follow,** and insisted that they follow His example. By all accounts of what we read in the New Testament, they followed the example Jesus set for them.

*John 13:15 **I have set you an** _____ **that you should*
*do as I have done for you.***

The Apostle Paul followed this same approach in his ministry by appealing to his disciples to follow his example in the same way as what he was following the example set by Jesus.

*1 Corinthians 11:1 **Follow my example**, as I follow **the example of*
Christ.
*Ephesians 5:1 **Follow God's example**, therefore, as dearly loved*
children

The Apostle Peter echoed this approach, both in exhorting Believers to follow Christ' example by following in His footsteps, and by exhorting us, as His under-Shepherds, to "***be examples.***"

*1 Peter 2:21 To this you were **called**, because **Christ** suffered for you,*
***leaving you an example**, that **you should follow in his steps**.*

Make a commitment in your life to be an example that others can follow.

Shepherds lead and guide their sheep.

Another way in which we provide for the flock entrusted to our care and watch is that **we** _____ **them** to "***green pastures and still waters***" and a place where their souls can be refreshed.

*Psalms 23:2-3 He makes me lie down in green pastures, **he leads me***
*beside quiet waters, he refreshes my soul. **He guides me** along*
the right paths for his name's sake.

Every opportunity we have to open the Word of God, read it together, hear what the Holy Spirit is saying to us, and how we may apply it to our lives, provide us with an opportunity to effectively care, protect and provide for our sheep. The Word restores us, refreshes us, guides us, leads us, and ultimately directs us.

> *Psalms 1:2-3 but whose delight is in the law of the Lord, and who meditates on his law, day and night. **That person is like a tree planted by streams of water**, which yields its fruit in season and whose leaf does not wither—whatever they do prospers.*

As Shepherds we lead our disciples to the green pastures of the Word, the green pastures of encounters in the Holy Spirit, and green pastures of building each other up through the gifts and power of the Holy Spirit. Nothing refreshes us like time spent in the Presence of God.

Conclusion

This session would not be concluded without us making a conscious decision to commit being such a purposeful Shepherd.

We explored together:

The Shepherd provides a caring environment within which they can practice protection and provision. We learned How best we may encourage and build each other up within the walls of this protected environment.

We also looked at How **Shepherds prayerfully protect their sheep by watching over them.** We protect and keep them by being spiritually alert and watchful in prayer. We also protect them by keeping them together as well as teaching them sound doctrine.

We looked at **providing our Disciples with an example to follow**, and finally at **committing to lead and guide** them along right paths and to places where their soul's would be refreshed.

> *"I pray that you will make a commitment to be that shepherd to provide such an example that others can follow. I pray that God will help us to*

keep and protect those entrusted to our care, "That none should perish." I also pray that we will have open hearts and minds to be spiritually alert and aware as to know what the Lord might be doing in our disciple's lives, to enable us to lead, guide, and protect them more efficiently. May God bless you in your pursuit of being the Best Shepherd you could ever be with the help of the precious Holy Spirit. Amen"

Assimilation Sheet for
The Purpose of a Shepherd

1. Complete the sentence. *The purpose of a Shepherd is to **care** for the sheep by _____ and _____ for them.*

2. Complete the sentence. *The best way to Disciple someone is to step up into the role of being a _____ for them.*

3. Complete the sentence. *The '_____' part is the most comprehensive and engaging part and requires the greatest level of _____ and endurance.*

4. Which Scripture particularly encourages us to provide a caring environment. _____

5. Name two ways in which we can encourage and build one another up. _____

_____

_____

6. Complete the sentence. *We protect them against _____ doctrines, _____ mindsets and destructive relationships and environments.*

7. What is the most efficient way to keeping watch over our disciples? Give a Scriptural reference from the life of Christ.

_____

_____

_____

8. Complete the sentence. Watching is _____ shepherding.

9. Shepherds protect their sheep. Which two pieces of equipment do they use and what is the purpose of each one of them?

_____

_____

_____

10. Jesus made three claims in His prayer in John 17 verse 12 What was His three claims?

_____

_____

_____

11. Give three Scriptures that exhorts us to protect our disciples by teaching them sound doctrine.

_____

_____

_____

12. The greatest legacy anyone can leave is their example. Provide some Scriptural support for this statement.

_____

_____

_____

13. What purpose does the Good Shepherd have in Psalms 23 verse 2-3?

_____

_____

_____

5
___

DEVELOPING DEEP AND MEANINGFUL RELATIONSHIPS

SESSION FIVE

The most effective part of Shepherding is *providing a place where people's lives could be _____, renewed, encouraged, and built up.*

This session is about **How to develop deep and meaningful _____** that will last the test of time. To enable us **to effectively disciple our disciples**, we, in the **first place**, need to be fully _____ **to shepherd and care** for those entrusted to our care, and **secondly, purpose-fully** _____ **deep and meaningful relationships** within which, **thirdly, true transformation** can take place, as well as where, **fourthly,** our disciples can ultimately **serve the purpose God** has for their lives.

Developing deep and meaningful relationships

We develop deep and meaningful relationships along a known pathway. **Understanding how to** responsibly pace oneself in **developing deep and meaningful relationships** will **help you to impact others** more **effectively.**

The ebb and flow of how we develop purposeful relationship requires **"know how"** as well as _____ **diligence.**

If you go deep too quickly you might find yourself at a **vulnerability beyond the depth of the relationship**, and that will unnecessarily expose you to getting hurt.

May your ministry in the Spirit and accompanied systematic equipping, form the solid base timeline along which you will pursue the development of lifelong relationships. To help us, let us look at a few key principles to helps us in our understanding.

JOHARI WINDOW

The Johari window is an **imaginary tool** we use to think about relationships. The _____ **Window** consist of **four quadrants**; each representing a different aspect and **dimension of how we are perceived** and **what people know about us**, and **what we know about ourselves**, and **how we relate to others.**

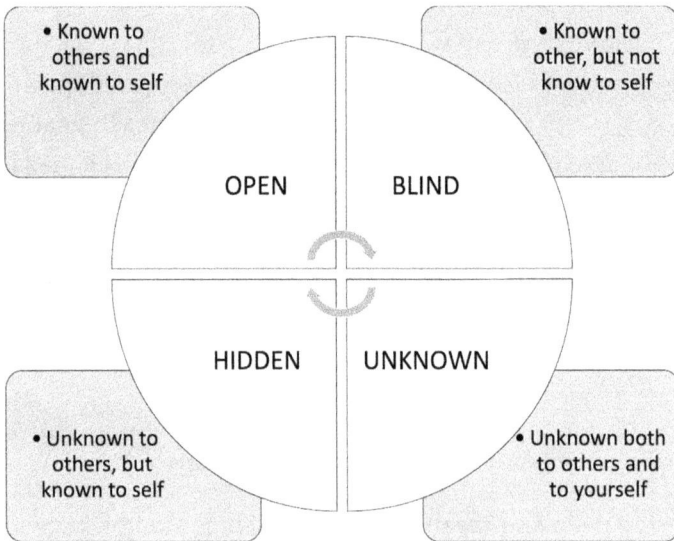

- Known to others and known to self
- Known to other, but not know to self

OPEN   BLIND

HIDDEN   UNKNOWN

- Unknown to others, but known to self
- Unknown both to others and to yourself

Johari Window Graphic

The JOHARI WINDOW brings to us an awareness that not everything we know about ourselves is known to others, but also, that others see and know things about us that we are not necessarily aware of.

There are four aspects to consider when developing self-awareness, both for ourselves and within those we are leading: the first is the **OPEN** area, then there is an area that is **HIDDEN** (undisclosed) by ourselves yet unknown to others, the third area represents what might be seen and known to others yet unknown to us, to which we are totally **BLIND** to, and finally there is an undiscovered and **UNKNOWN** area, within each one of us, not known to either ourselves, or others.

Let us explore them individually.

The OPEN dimension

The **OPEN dimension** to our lives represents that aspect of our lives that is _____ to both ourselves and by others. This could be **our Name**, the **colour of our eyes**, the **place we live in**, the **language** we speak, the **relationships** we have, our **education**, and our **beliefs.** Generally these are the things we choose to share with others, to varying degrees, as we will see later. This represents things that we are comfortable to share, or that might be known about us that is also known to others.

The HIDDEN dimension

The **HIDDEN dimension** represents that side of us where **we know things about ourselves** that is _____ **from the knowledge of others.** People might know you as an English-speaking person and assume that you are English, not knowing that you are actually a German-born Swede. Others might know you as a Brunette when in fact you are a blond. Other hidden things might represent your **belief-system, practices, habits, hobbies, education, heritage** or **preferences.** These might be **known to you** but **hidden from the sight or knowledge of others.**

The BLIND dimension

The BLIND dimension represents that side of our lives that **others see and know about us** that we are completely blind to. Others see and observe things in us, or about us which is _____ **to us.** They see behavioural patterns, attitudes and ways that might be apprehensible, yet we might be blind to the fact that we are behaving in unbecoming ways.

Before we were *"Born Again"* we spoke like the world, behaved and acted like the world, blinded to the fact that our sins blinded us from seeing how far away from God we've been and how apprehensible our conduct has been. Once we open ourselves to Jesus Christ, the blindfolds are removed, and we become aware of our sins and shortcomings.

There are areas or aspects of our lives, that we need to be open to, that others observe in and about us, to which we are currently blind to. Our journey with others should always bring within us *an awareness that the world does not only exist as we see or understand it*, and to *be open to learn and understand things better*, both about ourselves and about others. This aptitude will help us, and others, to grow together and develop deeper and more meaningful relationships.

UNKNOWN dimension

The UNKNOWN dimension represents *that part of our lives* to which *we have never woken up to* or *become aware of*, or discovered, *but the same is true for others* who come into a relationship with us. *The UNKNOWN dimension is unchartered and* _____ *territory for others as well as for us.*

The OBJECTIVE of understanding the Johari Window

The objective of understanding the **JOHARI** window is to *help us understand* the dynamics that is involved when we *lead people to self-discovery, openness, vulnerability and ultimate transformation.* This helps us understand that people might be *open in some areas* but *intentionally close in other areas*. Our journey into developing deep and meaningful, God-honouring relationships, will pursue ways in which we will *work on making the OPEN dimension larger* and the other areas smaller and smaller.

No deep relationship is possible if we do not open ourselves up to others, and at the same time allow others to help us become aware of possibilities to which we have been closed to before.

As Shepherds, we desire to help our disciples to become more like Jesus. We desire for them to open themselves up to the dream God has for them. We want to see people transformed by the power of the Holy Spirit. We desire to see them grow and develop and operate in ways that they never dreamt of. *We desire to see the Purposeful, Destined for Greatness Person discovered* and *unlocked*, and this require prayer, skill and intentional focus on the end goal.

Five levels of deepening relationships.

Another help in developing deep relationships is to have an understanding of the *Five levels of deepening relationships*. Let us explore the different levels of communicating. *The purpose is to help us learn* to understand *the pathway along which sound depths of relationships are developed*. This will both help us in understanding how to develop deeper relationships with our disciples along a responsible pathway, as well as to guide our disciples, through the various stages of developing the group, and their inter-relationships with each other, to do so in a responsible way.

If people disclose of themselves too quickly, they *make themselves vulnerable* beyond the level of relationship they've developed. This is dangerous and might lead to people exiting the group unnecessarily since they become uncomfortable with their premature disclosure. Disclosure is good, but only at a time when it is warranted and where the atmosphere for transformation is right. Let us look at the five levels:

Level 1 - Strangers - Speak and assess clichés

Level 2 - Acquaintances - Speak and assess facts

Level 3 - Friends - Share ideas and beliefs

Level 4 - Close Friends - Share emotions and feelings

Level 5 - Intimate Relationships - Share openly and full transparancy

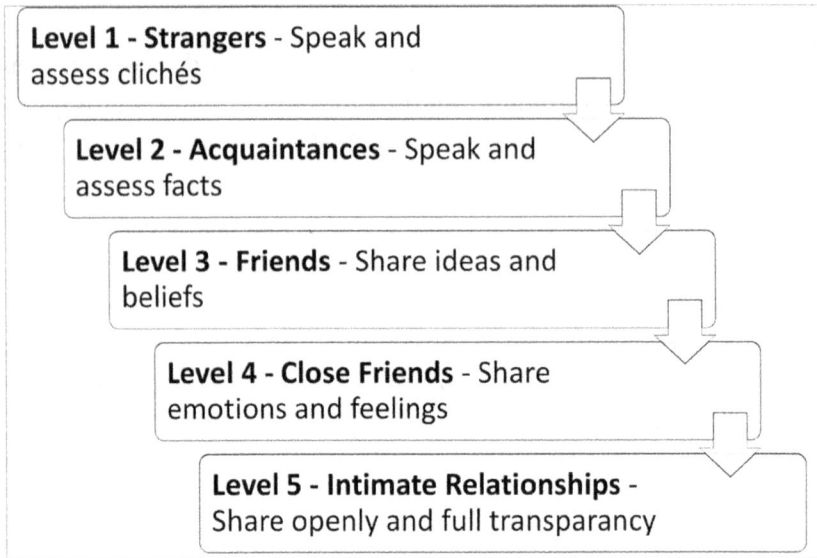

Diagram: Five levels of deepening relationships

Strangers – Speak clichés.

In the beginning of every relationship our conversations are based on _____. We hardly say anything meaningful except what is common knowledge. For example, "*It's hot,*" or "*the bus is full.*"

Acquaintances – Speak facts.

Once *we become acquainted* with people, the more *we speak verifiable* _____, in order that the relationship will develop. If facts do not stack up, the relationship will remain courteous but will never go deeper. Since *trust is one of the key essential ingredients* to good long-lasting relationship, it is imperative that you *ensure that what you communicate is true and factual.* Before people like or even love you for who you are, without knowing it, they assess you based on your words: *what you say, how you say it and the confidence with which you speak. If people trust the facts you share they most certainly will seek to keep and develop the relationship.*

Friends – Ideas and beliefs.

Once people go *from acquaintances to become known on a first name basis* and *mutual engagement is pursued,* *the sharing of* _____ *and* _____ *will be entertained.* If people *trust the facts you share,* they are *more likely to embrace the thought patterns of your ideas and beliefs.* This progressive sharing and entertaining of ideas and beliefs almost always predicates transformational and deeper relationships.

The potential to impact people's lives become greater at this point. The opportunity to lead people to transformation becomes greater at this point. *It requires,* beyond the sharing of your ideas and beliefs, *an intentional pursuit* of *"knowing the friend"* to ultimately equip them into their God purpose. Building purposeful relationships is of paramount importance if we desire to see lives _____ and *transformed.* No casual relationship has any real meaning or serve any purpose for life.

Close Friends - Share emotions and feelings.

Over time, as people entrench themselves into each other's lives, and for us towards seeing people grow in the Lord, maturing, and ultimately become Fathers and Mothers of Nations, the premium is to *stay focused on prayerfully developing the relationships deeper* so that we can ultimately together impact others for the advancement of the Gospel of Jesus Christ.

During this phase of developing deep and meaningful relationships we can move to a place where we should be able *share how we* _____ and *express our emotions* without guilt or a feeling of being guarded. If you trust someone whose ideas and beliefs you embrace then the natural next step is to let them into how you truly feel. This might be the expression of disappointment, gladness, fulfillment, love and even fear. As we share our emotions and feelings more freely, and receive appropriate and reciprocal response we will find the relationship deepen even more. If there is no reciprocation or appropriate response, as what you would expect from your sharing, then the likelihood of the relationship going deeper stalemates here.

Our goal is to help our disciples to develop deep and more meaningful relationship to enable them to bring transformation in their lives. When we become open and honest about our *hopes and dreams*, our *fears and failures*, we develop relationships for life. This phase draws people into becoming *more vulnerable and exposed*, however, if we've taken the cautious path of developing the relationship carefully, then true transformation will take place and people will be more likely changed and transformed into the likeness of Christ.

My caution is this: *never move or develop relationships beyond reciprocal open* _____ *and* _____.

Intimate Relationships – open and complete transparent relationships.

The deepest level of relationship is really reserved for covenantal relationships, or marriage to be more specific.

In developing these relationships, it is importance to know that the deeper the relationship level, the more transparency and therefor vulnerability will exist. *Transformation only exists along the pathway of becoming* _____ *and vulnerable.* As we help and guide our disciples along this pathway of disclosure, vulnerability and transformation their lives will be enriched, and the result will be a unified Body of Believers fulfilling the purpose of God for each of their lives.

Simultaneously, and alongside this pathway of developing deep and transformational relationships, there exist another dynamic that we need to be aware of and it is the *relationship cycle*.

```
        ┌─────────────┐
        │  Phase 1:   │
        │  History    │
        └─────────────┘
┌──────────────┐        ┌──────────────┐
│  Phase 4:    │        │ Phase 2: The │
│Transformation│        │  Challenge   │
└──────────────┘        └──────────────┘
        ┌─────────────┐
        │ Phase 3: The│
        │  Conflict   │
        └─────────────┘
```

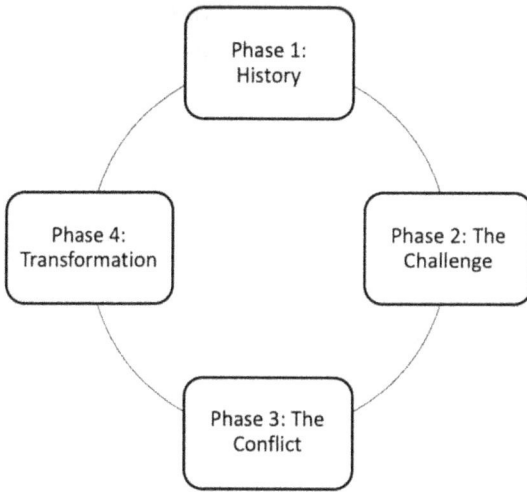

Relationships develop through cycles.

Phase 1: History

The first phase of building purposeful relationships is defined by the status quo; each one being his or her own person, seeing life and things from their *one-dimensional perspective*. This marks the starting point for each relationship.

In this phase, since we evangelise, we might start with *Level One and Level Two communication*. This phase is also identified by our pursuits to open up conversation with strangers. *We open conversations with sincere _____ and then by asking _____ questions to know them better.*

People open up quicker if we show *sincere interest in non-threatening situations*. Non-threatening situations are those where you will potentially part ways within minutes. If you are more likely to "bump" into these strangers more frequently then you *keep it consistent* and at a *low level of asking intruding questions*. They should, on the surface, seem casual, as if you are just showing interest. Remember, *we are engaging with strangers to find "men of peace'* with whom we can share Christ. We are looking for open hearts where it

seems that we could see ourselves build deep and meaningful relationships that would potentially advance the Kingdom of God
greatly.

When we bring our *"worthy men"* together for the first time, they
will start their joint relationship at this point as well. *Help them bridge
the unknown by communicating the things they have in common and
share.* It helps them connect in a positive atmosphere.

When *Philip brought Nicodemus to Jesus*, He made it easy by telling
him about Jesus. When Andrew left John the Baptist to follow Jesus,
he took his brother along. On both of these occasions the disciples
prepared the way for their "friends and family" to meet the Lord. In
one sense we need to do the same when building our discipleship
groups.

> *John 1:41-42 The first thing Andrew did was to find his brother
> Simon and tell him, "We have found the Messiah" (that is, the
> Christ). 42 And he brought him to Jesus. Jesus looked at him
> and said, "You are Simon son of John. You will be called
> Cephas" (which, when translated, is Peter).*

> *John 1:43, 45 The next day Jesus decided to leave for Galilee. Finding
> Philip, he said to him, "Follow me." 45 Philip found Nathanael
> and told him, "We have found the one Moses wrote about in
> the Law, and about whom the prophets also wrote—Jesus of
> Nazareth, the son of Joseph."*

The beginning of establishing a relationship is for the most part
easy, unless you just don't connect with the people you are pursuing.
On both of these occasions we see that the common denominator
was one's knowledge of Jesus, and then sharing it with the other.

*Sharing something _____ about those whom
you're introducing to each other, always sets a good positive departure
point to starting new relationships.* Jesus immediately connected with
those who were introduced to Him, by ministering to them by the
Holy Spirit. We need to be constantly tuned into the Holy Spirit to

connect with people more effectively. *Divine connections has the capacity to catapult relationships deep within one or two encounters.*

Phase 2: The Challenge

The second phase of building purposeful relationships is where things become a little trickier as *we become aware of what we like and don't like about the other person.* If we could keep in the forefront of our minds the reason why we felt to start and pursue the specific relationship, it will help us to develop "that" person. *During this phase people are _____ and often have a sense of being challenged.*

- We are challenged _____ by observing the *different values* people uphold.
- We are challenged by *what people endorse* and see as *normal behaviour.*
- We are challenged by people's _____ *status.*
- We are challenged by *our own emotional adaptabilities.*
- We are challenged by *other's habits, practices and sayings.*
- We are challenged by *the way people respond to _____ circumstances.*
- We are challenged _____ as we face our own short comings and need of God.
- We are challenged as *we come to know the purpose God has for our lives.*
- We are challenged as *we become aware of the changes that is required* to obey God.
- We are also challenged when we consider *how much time we wasted in not following God.*

During this phase we open ourselves up, by becoming more transparent and vulnerable. It is this openness that challenges us as we come to terms with how vulnerable it's making us. One of the areas we are challenged in, on the pathway of openness and vulnerability, is towards *being transformed into the likeness of Christ. We,* of necessity, *have to confront the challenge* to our upbringing, our values, cultural habits and practices, and this leads to *the next phase of conflict*.

Whenever *we are challenged in our beliefs, behavior and thought patterns*, we become aware that much of *our adamic nature is in opposition to sound biblical wisdom*, and that brings us to *a Gospel Conflict which needs resolving with the help of the Holy Spirit* and *a Good Shepherd*. We are often confronted with our sins and how it has impacted our lives. We are confronted with how we lived our lives, and thought it was right and normal, just to discover that it was wrong.

These things bring us to a confrontation of who we are and how change is required to become the people we want to become, and what God want us to be. The constant agent working primarily in us is *the Holy Spirit* who brings on this confrontation, or conviction. *A conviction calls for change.* When the Holy Spirit convicts us of sin in our lives, it calls us to change our ways.

> *John 16:8 When he comes, **he will convict the world of guilt in regard to sin** and righteousness and judgment:*

When the Apostle Paul wrote to the *Thessalonians*, he addressed them on a number of issues which *brought deep conviction within them*.

> *1 Thessalonians 1:5 because our gospel came to you not simply with words, but also with power, with **the Holy Spirit** and with **deep conviction**. You know how we lived among you for your sake.*

Phase 3: Conflict

Any challenge of our values, habits, behavior, beliefs and knowledge always is followed by a period of _____. The outcome of conflict determines the values, practices and behaviours we will uphold or adapt to in our lives. This conflict is often more on *a spiritual level* than on a physical level. Depending on the depth of our *upheld mindsets*, the *conflict might be a more painful experience* in one area than in other parts of our lives where we can more easily *observe the wisdom towards change and transformations.*

We always need to remind ourselves of what Scripture teaches us.

> *Ephesians 6:12 For **our struggle is not against flesh and blood**, but against the rulers, against the authorities, against the powers of this dark world and against the spiritual forces of evil in the heavenly realms.*

> *2 Corinthians 10:3-6 For though we live in the world, **we do not wage war as the world does**. The weapons we fight with are not the weapons of the world. On the contrary, they have divine power to demolish strongholds. We demolish arguments and every pretension that sets itself up against the knowledge of God, and we take captive every thought to make it obedient to Christ. And we will be ready to punish every act of disobedience, once your obedience is complete.*

This spiritual conflict, fought with spiritual weapons and armament, aligns us with the Will and Purpose of God. The hope is that *conviction brings us to a place of obedience to God* and the favor of God. For some, conviction could come in a moment of prayer and contemplation in the Word, for others it might be more of a process.

Transformation takes place through conflict.

Our purpose as Shepherds is to help our disciples through this phase of conflict. *Never make their conflict your conflict, neither trivialise the conflict* and trauma they might experience in *"letting go"* or "leaving" things of the past behind. *Never take it personal* as they might vent themselves in the process of trying to come to terms with the change that is required to grow in their faith and stature in Christ. *Without being challenged*, through the Word, the Holy Spirit, or through us, as we share the Truths of God's Word to our disciples, *no change or trans-formation is possible.*

The Apostle Paul wrote to the church in Corinth and emphasised the way in which they were challenged by his letter, but more importantly the conviction it brought and ultimate transformation in their character and ministry, was clearly observed. This is what we are trusting God for in our disciples.

> *2 Corinthians 7:8-12 **Even if I caused you sorrow by my letter, I do not regret it.** Though I did regret it–I see that my letter hurt you, but only for a little while – 9 yet now I am happy, not because you were made sorry, but because **your sorrow led you to repentance.** For you became sorrowful as God intended and so were not harmed in any way by us. 10 **Godly sorrow brings repentance that leads to salvation** and leaves no regret, but worldly sorrow brings death. 11 **See what this godly sorrow has produced in you:** what earnestness, **what eagerness to clear yourselves,** what indignation, what alarm, what longing, what concern, **what readiness to see justice done.** At every point you have proved yourselves to be innocent in this matter.*

This conviction is nothing more than a major conflict which results in godly sorrow and repentance, and ultimately a transformed life.

Phase 4. Transformation

Phase four is defined by being transformed in your life. I learned about transformers at school. Transformers take one kind of electricity from one source and transform it to another form and consistency out on the other end. *Transformation takes place when we input our old selves as clay into the hands of the Almighty God,* submits to him, allowing Him to form us and creating something beautiful of our lives.

"Transformation is the process by which our old nature, encompassing our will, intellect, emotions, values, habits, ambitions and practices is transformed by a combined process of submitting our own selves, with willingness to permanently change, together with desiring the Holy Spirit to bring the sanctification and renewed creation forth on the other end."

Once we come to a place of conviction, as those led by the Holy Spirit, and constantly under Him working consecration in us, we repent, we change, and we turn for good. This change is called *transformation*.

> *2 Corinthians 7:11 NIV 11 **See what this godly sorrow has produced in you:** what earnestness, what eagerness to clear yourselves, what indignation, what alarm, what longing, what concern, what readiness to see justice done. At every point you have proved yourselves to be innocent in this matter.*

God has our best interest at heart, and so should we for those who we lead and care for during their transformation process. **Constantly remind yourself**, and those you lead, of the goal before us. *Let us keep our eyes focused on the goal of becoming and being like Jesus.*

> *Philippians 2:5 **Your attitude should be the same** as that of Christ Jesus:*

> *Philippians 3:10 **I want to know Christ** and the power of his resurrection and the fellowship of sharing in his sufferings, **becoming like him** in his death,*

Change for good

This kind of change is good, *it makes us better people*, and **better people to be around with**. This kind of change presents Jesus to others in a real and transferable way. This change brings about *change in our speech, actions, behavior and reactions.*

Transformation

Our goal is to see people transformed in their person, character and nature. *We desire to equip them with every good thing that will lead them to be fully transformed until Christ is formed in them.*

> Romans 12:2 *Do not conform to the pattern of this world but* **be transformed by the renewing of your mind.** *Then you will be able to test and approve what God's will is —his good, pleasing and perfect will.*

> 2 Corinthians 3:18 *And we all, who with unveiled faces contemplate the Lord's glory, are* **being transformed into his image** *with ever-increasing glory, which comes from the Lord, who is the Spirit.*

The purpose of transformation is that Christ is formed in us. Our work as Shepherds is to help our disciples to be transformed until Christ is formed in them.

> Galatians 4:19 *My dear children, for whom I am again in the pains of childbirth* **until Christ is formed in you,**

The Apostle Paul speaks of God's goal and means of seeing His people equipped and mobilised for service. *We are so much more effective in building the Church up when we are mature and Christ formed in us.*

> Ephesians 4:12 **His intention was the perfecting and the full equipping of the saints** *(His consecrated people), [that they should do] the work of ministering toward building up Christ's body (the church),*

Romans 8:29 For those God foreknew he also predestined to ***be***
*   **conformed to the image of his Son,** that he might be the*
*   firstborn among many brothers and sisters.*

1 Corinthians 15:49 And just as we have borne the image of the
*   earthly man, **so shall we bear the image of the heavenly man.***

God desires that we bear the image of His Son just as we borne the image of our adamic nature. This is possible with the Power of the Holy Spirit.

*"**Transformation takes place when we combine being vulnerable,**
transparent and humble, with a _____ **and openness to**
_____ **and be renewed into the person God dreamed us to be.**"*

Vulnerability and transparency

One of **the greatest expressions of vulnerability and transparency is when we confess our sins to God.** When we are in a caring Shepherding relationship and confess our sins, it provides opportunity for change and transformation to takes place.

*James 5:16 Therefore, **confess your sins to each other** and pray for*
*   each other so that you may be healed. The prayer of a righteous*
*   person is powerful and effective.*

*Acts 19:18 Many of those who believed now came and **openly***
*   **confessed what they had done.***

It takes great humility to say to your "shepherd" that you have sinned, and that you need help and forgiveness. It requires a loving and accepting environment where you can be held accountable to turn from wicked ways and practices. As Shepherds of God, we desire to see our disciples turn from worldly ways to walk in godly, exemplary ways.

So, step one is to keep the focus clear in our hearts and minds, that we serve as His Servants to equip our disciples to be transformed into the likeness of Christ Jesus. To do this efficiently, *we need to create an environment where people can be vulnerable and transparent,* but also where they can be held *accountable, to ensure they truly change and transform into the people God desires them to be.*

Built up

Our goal is defined: that *the Body be built up in Him*!

> *Ephesians 4:12-13 "to prepare God's people for works of service, so that the body of Christ may be built up until we all reach unity in the faith and in the knowledge of the Son of God and become mature, attaining to the whole measure of the fullness of Christ."*

Our prayer is that you will grow in understanding these simple, yet powerful skills to assist you to help your disciples develop deep and kingdom advancing relationships.

Assimilation Sheet for
Developing deep and meaningful Relationships

1. Complete the statement. *The most effective part of Shepherding is providing a place where people's lives could be* _____, *renewed, encouraged, and built up.*

2. Complete the sentence. *The ebb and flow of how we develop purposeful relationship requires "know how" as well as* _____ *diligence.*

3. Name the four quadrants of the Johari Window, and briefly explain the importance of each aspect for us to consider in developing deep and meaningful relationships.

- _____
- _____
- _____
- _____

4. What is the objective to understanding the Johari Window?

_____
_____
_____

5. Name the Five levels of deepening relationships, and provide a brief description for each level.

- _____
- _____
- _____
- _____
- _____

6. Complete the sentence. *We open conversations with sincere* _____ *and then by asking* _____ *questions to know them better.*

. . .

7. Complete the sentence. *Sharing something* _____ *about those whom you're introducing to each other, always sets a good positive departure point to starting new relationships.*

8. Name a few areas in which we often find ourselves challenged when we develop new relationships.

- _____
- _____
- _____
- _____
- _____
- _____
- _____
- _____

9. Which are the four phases of relationship building?

- _____
- _____
- _____
- _____

10. Complete the sentence. *Any challenge of our values, habits, behavior, beliefs and knowledge always is followed by a period of* _____.

11. Define the process of Transformation.

_____
_____
_____
_____

12. What is the purpose of transformation? Give Scriptural support for your answer.

_____
_____
_____

13. Complete the sentence. *"Transformation takes place when we combine being vulnerable, transparent and humble, with a _____ and openness to _____ and be renewed into the person God dreamed us to be."*

6

PRACTICAL KEYS

SESSION SIX

T his session will provide us with practical ways to lead a group
effectively and efficiently.

Meeting Place setup.

Set out the meeting place in a _____ as opposed to a classroom
setting. Make sure that you have a comfortable amount of seating
available for everyone. Preferably, no one should sit at a lower level
than others. If your culture is comfortable to be seated on the floor,
then make room that everyone sits on the floor. If your culture sits on
chairs, make sure that everyone sits within a reasonable height to
each other, and that *everyone can see everyone else in the room.* We
encourage open and transparent communication and this arrangement
will assist in helping people to be open and *free to minister to each
other*, as well as to observe and share together.

WWM's

Once we bring our disciples together in a group, there are a number
of practical keys that will assist us to coordinate these gatherings in

an orderly and functional way. There is something that is now commonly known as the WWM's for effective group functioning. The **WWM's stand for: Welcome, Worship, Ministry, and Word, Witness, Mission.** These four W's and 2 M's form the broad outline for our *60-90 minutes together as a group.* Let us look at these 6 integrated parts for leading an effective group encounter.

Welcome.

1. Personally Welcome people to your house.

Welcome people as they arrive to your house. It is preferable that _____ meet your guests at the door. It shows that you value them.

- Ask them how they are?
- Ask them about their day?
- Ask them how they feel?
- Ask them follow up questions about their family's welfare? Always start with the person and then branch out to the immediate family and other circumstances.

2. Connect people during this time.

Use this welcoming time to help the group to be better _____ with each other as well, especially in the beginning phase of them meeting together.

- **Friendliness** - The purpose is to make them feel welcome and that you feel blessed that they are there. Remember, we want to shepherd them through the Word, by the Holy Spirit Gifts and through natural means. We are blessed to have people come to us. Treat them with honor and respect their time and effort.
- **Hospitality** - One of the best ways to show hospitality is to offer them something to _____. The purpose is not to

have a tea drinking party, but just a way of showing hospitality and to let people settle in and relax. It is just to make people feel relaxed and welcome. Even a glass of water will work.

3. Officially, Welcome Everyone.

Draw all the various conversations to a close, once all your expected guests have arrived, by *raising your _____ slightly* and *welcoming them all* for coming. Always declare your gathering open by saying something expectant and positive. *"I am so excited for this time together. I believe the Holy Spirit is really going to minister to each one of us today,"* or *"I have been so blessed with the Word today. I look forward to sharing God's Word with us today,"* Or *"We are so blessed to be able to gather together, and to share this time together as friends."*

The purpose of this process of welcoming is to *help people relax, forget about the challenges, struggles,* and *concerns of their day,* and *settle in* on the purpose of them being there.

Welcoming people sincerely *opens their hearts to you and to God.*

4. Opening Prayer

It is always a great idea to open every gathering in prayer to set the tone and affirm the purpose for coming together. You might want to open your gatherings with prayer or ask one or more of your group to open in prayer. The purpose of this time of prayer is to welcome the Lord in your midst, and to commit your hearts to worship Him, to Hear from Him, to avail yourselves to be instruments through whom He may minister to build and encourage others.

Worship.

Declare your purpose for worshipping together.

Immediately after welcoming and praying, draw the attention of your people to *the purpose* of your gathering, which is to *Worship God, Hear from Him, Learn from Him, and committing yourselves unto His service.*

Leading worship

Very few people actually have confidence in leading worship, so, if you have someone to lead the group in a time of singing songs of worship, count yourself highly fortunate. For the rest of us, we have to prepare to lead the singing of *2-3 songs* that is focused on bringing our praise and adoration to Jesus. You can use *worship music from your Christian Music collection* if it could be done seamlessly.

Make Worship simple.

My advice is to *make it as natural as possible*, because worship should not only be done when we gather together, *we should be worshippers of God everyday* of our lives. Singing *Accapella* (without music - voices only) is good. It helps people to hear their own voices as they worship God.

Heart-felt Worship

Worship should come from our hearts to touch the heart of God. Our time in Worship is devoted so that we can focus on Him, His Spirit and His Word. We want to *open our hearts and minds to Him.*

Be considerate in your worship

Be respectful when you meet in places where there are other people living in close vicinity to where you meet. In other words, don't sing so loud that you unnecessarily draw unwanted attention to your singing as to put people off at your inconsiderate worship. Worship should be done *at the same level as what you would present it to God during your own quiet times of Worship.*

Ensure people connect with God in Worship.

Ensure that the worship *leads people to connect with God.* As the Leader of the group, you should always be prayed up before every group meeting so that you could lead worship by your example, even though the person who is supposed to lead the worship might not be.

Remember that *the time of worship is to set the atmosphere for a time of ministry* to the people and between each other.

Sing from your heart and focus your attention on Him.

> John 4:23-24 *"Yet a time is coming and has now come when the true worshipers will worship the Father in spirit and truth, for they are the kind of worshipers the Father seeks. God is spirit, and his worshipers must worship in spirit and in truth."*

Focus on the Nature and Character of God in Worship.

One of the ways to lead worship is to choose a theme on the _____ and _____ of God, and then worship God in song accordingly. Another way is to choose Scripture Songs, especially those we learned from the _____. They are often easy to learn and to remember. The purpose is to help the group give expression of their love and devotion to God, in song.

Ministry.

The time of ministry is one of the most impacting times of every meeting since *the needs of the people are met* by the _____ *of the Holy Spirit.*

Be an Instrument of God

Prepare to be an instrument through whom the Holy Spirit can meet the spiritual needs of your people. The Apostle Paul taught us that he desired to meet together, to impart some Spiritual gift to strengthen and encourage the believers. We should do the same during this time of ministry.

> Romans 1:11-12 "11 I long to see you so **that I may impart to you some spiritual gift to make you strong**– 12 that is, that you and I may be mutually encouraged by each other's faith."

Allow the Gifts of the Holy Spirit to operate.

May the Gifts of the Holy Spirit be used to build each other up. Be an example and encourage the group to minister to each other in an orderly way.

If you centre your time together around Jesus, the Word and His Holy Spirit, then He will build them up in their faith. Remember, we want more of Him in our lives!

This time of ministry will provide comfort, care, direction, encouragement and instruction.

Limit lone Rangers

Don't let any one-person minister alone or primarily. If there is to be that one person, it will be you, however, your goal is to encourage your group, who should all be filled with the Holy Spirit, and have discovered their spiritual gifts at some point in conclusion of them doing the Spiritual Gifts discovery weekend encounter.

Body ministry is key during this time.

Facilitate this time. Don't force it, however, lead by your example. Ministry time is not spiritual counseling. It is hearing what the Holy

Spirit is saying to His people.

Encourage

Encourage one another. Build each other up.

Drawing Ministry Time to a Close.

Draw the ministry time to a *close by* _____, as might be appropriate to share, what the Lord did and said during this time. It is always an easier way to draw this ministry time to a *close with a* _____ *of thanksgiving* that you lead.

Word.

Hearing and receiving the Word

Ministry time should *lead into hearing and receiving the Word* of the Lord.

Receiving instruction in the Word

During the Word time we initially, primarily teach our disciples the Discipleship Foundation Series materials from Step One and Step Two.

* **Note to the teacher!** *During this weekend encounter phase, we unpack and internalise the weekend encounter material, especially how we might put it into practice. It will be advantageous if you prepare a suitable "Word" from some previous Step's material during this time.*

You are the initial sharer of the Word

During the teaching of Step 1 and 2 you will most certainly be the Primary Discipler. This might take you the better part of 6 months to complete. During the initial 6-9 months of your group meeting, you will be the primary teacher.

Directive to Facilitative

In the *initial stage You will be highly* _____ *during this teaching time*, however, as your disciples put things into practice and lead their own groups, you will find that a transition will take place as you provide a Word of encouragement to them, and then application to them fulfilling the call of God on their lives. *The goal is for you to become more of a facilitator.*

Remember, we want to see our disciples become fully mature followers of Jesus. We desire to see that they hear from God clearly, and that they put into practice the very things they were taught. The only way that this is possible in this regard is to intentionally transition from leading in a highly directive way to becoming more of a leader who walk alongside your disciples as they put things into practice. This *"walking alongside"* is called facilitation.

Putting it into practice

It is essential that we always remember that our discussions around the Word should always culminate into the: *How can I put this into practice in my life?* If there be any sharing let it be the confession of commitment to putting it into practice.

This is *not a time for arguments or opinions* to be aired. The Word time should neither be a time of disciplining.

Let it be centered on the Bible

Our discussions should always be based on what the Word of God teaches. It is a time to learn the Word of God. *The Bible form the backbone of all the Discipleship material* we developed. Keep it void from self-interpretation and rather, like a child, receive the Word of God as God gave it to us.

Witness

Testify

Draw the Word time to a *close by asking people to* _____ of what the Lord did for them during that meeting. Testimonies build people's faith as they hear, and proclaim, what the Lord has done for them.

One Minute testimonies

Share one-minute testimonies. Make sure that you get as many testimonies in as possible. It is sometimes easier to get people to share for one minute than to get them to share at all. It both offers a comfortable space and timing within to share as well as limit those who might cease an opportunity to take the floor.

Moderating sharing

It does happen at times that someone might extend the *one-minute time restriction.* Just be wise whether to allow it or to draw their testimony to a close. One of the best ways is to step in and say something like: *"Wow, its amazing what the Lord did for you, let's hear from .... I see they are equally excited to share today."*

Testifying brings liberty

When people learn the value of sharing what the Lord did or do for them, *they become more liberated to share outside* the group with others about the Lord's goodness.

Testifying activates awareness of what God is doing

This exercise *brings a greater awareness, appreciation and recognition of the work of God* in our lives. People become much more aware of the work of God in their own lives as they hear the testimonies from others sharing.

Encourage everyone to share

Some will be more open to share than others. Our role is to draw people into sharing by highlighting to them what they sensed God did for them. *Get them to see it for themselves.* Initially we have to point it out to them, but later you will see them responding to this by themselves spontaneously.

Mission

We *conclude* our *60-90 minutes together* with *casting* _____ *of our mission.* It is easy to ramble off the mission part, however, getting the group to take a moment to share in groups of two or three on the main areas where they can prayerfully trust the Lord to work in and through them, usually activates the Vision into them being on mission with God.

Prayer transitions our intentions into active participation

The *true impact* of *declaring our mission comes* when we *put action to our words of confession by* _____ for, and with each other. The first, and *primary activity* to see any *Mission accomplished*, is when we unite our hearts to approach the Throne of God in *praying for it.*

- Our mission is to *seek and save the lost,* so, let the group form sub-groups of 3-4 and pray for each other's lost people to be saved.
- Our mission is to *make disciples of all nations,* so, in these groups pray for each other that God will bless each one with *the worthiest people to disciple,* to advance the Kingdom of God.
- Our mission is to *preach the gospel,* so, pray for boldness to

be able to *use every opportunity to share your faith* with outsiders.

- Our mission is to *be examples for others to follow*, so, we pray for each other that we will be worthy examples, *open letters*, that will present Christ in a worthy manner.

Close every discipleship gathering by reiterating the Mission God called us to.

Afterword

In conclusion, we need to be good stewards of our time together. Let us take a few moments and look at the recommended timelines within which to accomplish all of these six key elements to conclude a dynamically impacting meeting.

Timelines for gatherings

Welcome

The welcome should not extend over 10-15 minutes. The longer it takes, the harder it will be to refocus the attention of the people. *Let people arrive around 5 minutes prior to the set time,* and *welcome people on time so that we show respect for those who came on time.* If you slack on starting time, you might find that the worthiest of people will stop coming since the likelihood that you will then also run over time will be there.

The *rule of thumb* is this: *the more worthier the people are that you minister to, the more likely they will be to follow a disciplined timeline.* Honor them since they are more likely to be able to teach other.

Worship

The worship time can be 10-15 minutes and should flow into

Ministry time seamlessly.

Ministry

Ministry should be done in a 10-15-minute timeframe, so that you could have a good 30 minutes to share the Word, or Teaching, for the day.

Word

Give yourself 30 minutes to teach the Word with enough time afterwards to discuss and internalise the Word or Teaching.

Witness

Give 5 minutes for people to share their testimonies of what the Lord did for them during their time together.

Mission

Secure at least 5-10 minutes at the end of your gathering time *to allow your people to pray with each other*, as well as to embrace their calling and mission together. If you overrun on other parts you will find people take the opportunity to excuse themselves during this vital conclusion.

This is probably the part that will catapult your disciples most into their mission and purpose for God. It *brings a sense of responsibility and mutual accountability* when they share and pray together.

If you can keep all of this under 90 minutes, then you will see great fruit from your good stewardship.

In Conclusion

In conclusion of this session, let us address two more essential elements which helps us immensely in leading our groups well:

Hospitality

Many *groups love socialising* after meetings, however, do not let this be the norm. *Rather meet on other occasions for fellowship and meals.* We all live in a time-constraint environment where every minute counts, therefor let us make the expectation clear that people don't feel rude or unsocial for not lingering beyond the 90 minutes.

There are always those who want to remain behind to further unpack or assimilate the happenings of the time together. We as Shepherds need to be prepared for it, and somehow welcome those moments as people come closer to Jesus, and their hearts more open to His Will and purpose.

Discipline

Sometimes we are required to bring correction to people who acted in an unacceptable way or manner, either themselves or to others during a meeting. If the opportunity arises then *ask them to meet with you during a mutually convenient time* to discuss the incident or occasion.

Discipline in private, Praise in public

Most *sheep are open to such correction and guidance.* Goats are never open to instruction and discipline. Remember, these are God's people who devoted their lives to Christ, and you are leading them on His behalf. *Remind them* that *you are there to care* for them, and that *their behavior or actions either advance or thwart the purpose of God*, both in their lives, as well as in the lives of the rest of the group. *Discipline in private* as far as is possible and appropriate. *Praise in public!*

Finally, enjoy the meetings, since it is here that you will see strangers become the family of God. It is here that you will observe the Grace of God in action. It is here with them that you will grow and mature in your faith and reliance on the Holy Spirit. *Enjoy!*

Assimilation Sheet for
The Practical Keys

1. Complete the sentence. *Set out the meeting place in a* _____ *as opposed to a classroom setting.*

2. What does the acronym WWM represent? _____
_____
_____

3. Which are the four main ingredients to Welcoming well?
_____
_____
_____
_____

4. Complete the sentence. *The purpose of this process of welcoming is to help people* _____, *forget about the challenges, struggles, and* _____ *of their day, and settle in on the purpose of them being there. Welcoming people* _____ *opens their hearts to you and to* ____.

5. Complete the sentence. *The purpose of your gathering, is to* _____ *God, Hear from Him,* _____ *from Him, and committing yourselves unto His* _____.

6. How do we know that it is the Will of God to take time to Worship? Provide a Scripture for your answer.
_____
_____
_____

7. What happens during the Ministry time, and by whose ministry?
_____
_____

8. Body ministry is important during ministry time. Which Scripture exhorts us towards Body ministry? _____

9. There are two keys parts to closing the ministry time. How do we draw the Ministry time to a close?
_____

10. There is an intentional transition that needs to take place in How we teach and equip our disciples during the Word time. How are we teaching initially and where do we intend to transition to?

_____

_____

_____

_____

11. Which are two essential parts and focuses during the Word part?

_____

_____

12. During the Witness time of our meetings, How long should we encourage the testimonies to be? _____

13. Name possible outcomes from this witnessing time?

_____

_____

_____

_____

14. Complete the sentence. *The true impact of declaring our mission comes when we put action to our words of confession by* _____ *for, and with each other.*

15. Name the four primary focuses of our Mission.

_____

_____

_____

_____

16. Provide the suggested time allocation for each of the essential focuses of a group meeting.

1. Welcoming -_____

2. Worship -_____

3. Ministry -_____

4. Word -_____

5. Witness -_____

6. Mission -_____

17. Complete the sentence. *It brings a sense of responsibility and* _____ *accountability when they share and* _____ *together.*

   18. Complete the sentence. *Discipline in* _____ *and Praise in* _____ *!*

7

PRACTICAL APPLICATION
SESSION SEVEN

L eading a group is quite a challenging exercise which requires some understanding as well. In this final session we will look at two additional practical areas: *The Equipping process* as well as *the _____ of forming a cohesive well-functioning group*. Both are equally essential for our understanding as well as keeping us sane during the tumultuous times that we all go through when we bring people from different backgrounds and values together, especially when it is to disciple them as Christ followers.

Equipping Process

The *equipping process* deals with the *intentional equipping* towards *transitioning _____ and accountability* from ourselves to those we lead and care for. This is a particularly delicate process to lead, mostly adult people, from spiritually infancy to be fully mature followers of Christ.

As with children, during their *initial few years*, the relationship is led by us being *highly directive and instructive*. As our children *grow up*, we hold them *increasingly accountable* to hold their own. We initially brush their teeth, but after a while we teach them to brush it with our supervision, and still later, for many years in some cases, we have to ask them daily whether they brushed their teeth. There is a point though that this is no longer required under normal circumstances. This initial highly directive stage of instruction does not define us as controlling and manipulating, it is simply an essential role we need to play since we care for our children's well-being.

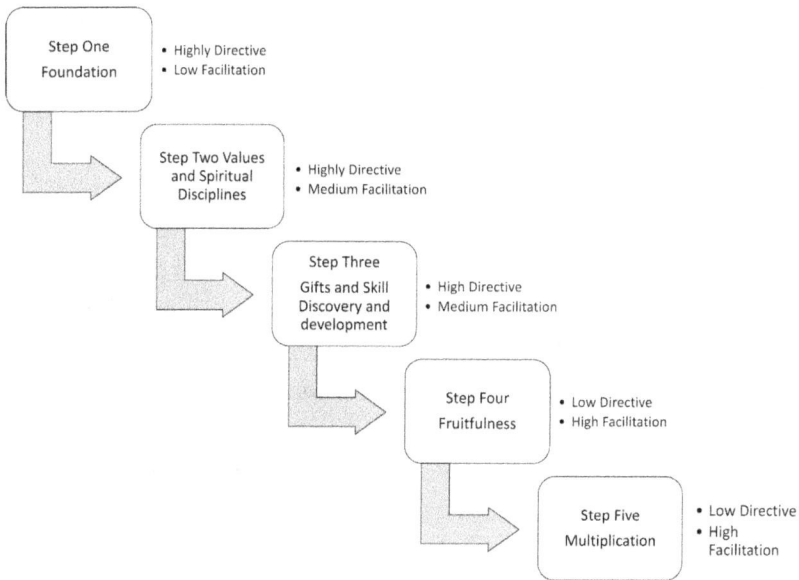

Equipping Process within the Five Discipleship Steps

The discipleship process develops from an initial ***highly directive*** and no facilitation approach, to ultimately relating with ***low directive*** instruction and ***high facilitation***.

Directive Learning

Directive – meaning that you ***direct the course of thought***. You instruct with a high sense of sharing irrefutable truth, meaning it is not up for discussion.

When we use directive learning, we equip our disciples by

teaching them the principles of God's Word, both by sharing the principles from God's Word, but more importantly by giving them a living example, through application in your own life. *In directive learning we _____, we _____ and we direct the course of learning and understanding.*

Facilitative Learning

Facilitation – meaning that you *provide more emphasised _____, by asking open-ended and _____ questions*, on how to apply the contents, more than on the information that is shared for assimilation.

For true transformation to take place in this equipping process we need to place a higher priority on creating and providing an example from whom others can learn, than being a conveyor of new information. This learning aspect through this equipping process is *more caught than taught*. It should be *seen and observed firsthand* for this to be effectively communicated, understood and received by others.

> *2 Timothy 1:5 I have been reminded of your **sincere faith, which first lived in** your grandmother Lois **and in your mother** Eunice and, I am persuaded, **now lives in you also.***

The things that the Apostle Paul encouraged his spiritual son, Timothy, to teach was alive and observed by other in his family, and in him also. He was encouraged to teach the word but also with the emphasis to be an example to the Believers. Repeatedly we read about '*teaching*' and '*my way of life*' in the same phrase or sentence. These were coupled and this should be our approach as well.

> *2 Timothy 3:10 You, however, **know all about my teaching, my way of life**, my purpose, faith, patience, love, endurance,*

> *1 Timothy 4:11-13 11 **Command and teach these things**. 12 Don't let anyone look down on you because you are young, but **set an***

example for the believers in speech, in life, in love, in faith and in purity. 13 Until I come, devote yourself to the public reading of Scripture, to preaching and to teaching.

*1 Timothy 4:15-16 15 Be diligent in these matters; **give yourself wholly to them, so that everyone may see your progress. 16 Watch your life and doctrine closely.** Persevere in them, because if you do, you will save both yourself and your hearers.*

Nothing impacts others as much as a _____ *example.* We command and teach these things since they live in us.

Directive Process

When we start the Discipleship journey with new Believers, especially during **Step One and Two** where we **give them instruction** in **building a solid foundation** for their faith, as well as teach them the **Values of the Kingdom of God** and **Spiritual Disciplines** to maintain their growth and development in the Lord, **our approach** is to **provide highly directive instruction.** This highly directive approach will be appreciated and followed when we model the very things we teach. **The more visible our directive teaching can be observed** in our lives, **the more our teaching will impact** those whom we lead in the Lord.

When we proceed to **Step Three in the Discipleship process,** we equip them along *a shared pathway of instruction and* _____. We teach them and facilitate them to discover and develop ways to **put into practice what they learn,** especially as it relates to others. The key in this Step of Discipleship is that we not only equip them with skills but also with an understanding towards future implementation. It is therefore important to **add greater facilitation** during these **weekend equipping encounters** in order that the disciples will not just think on how it benefits them but also how they will help their disciples to grow.

Step Four and Five are low directive since we are working with **disciples who have become friends,** co-labourers and partners in advancing the Kingdom of God. We have *a low directive approach of equipping* since the emphasis is *leaning more towards encouragement* towards a being a better example and at the same time equipping your disciples with *skill sharpening tools* and *keeping them focused* on keeping intentionally focused on the task at hand. *The directive part is decreasing* as your *disciples assume their personal relationship with the Holy Spirit*, who is the ultimate teacher of us all.

We remain their Shepherds, and as such, we will always continue to lead them in their walk with God. *We will always provide care, guidance, protection and provision* for their growth and well-being, and this is where there will always remain *a low-directive component*. On the whole, effective leading at this stage of our disciple's growth, *facilitation is key*.

Facilitation Process

The facilitation only become of essence once you have given instruction in the ways, *principles* and *values of the Kingdom of God*. Once your disciples have been taught in an area, then only does the facilitation process start.

Open-ended Questions

The Facilitation process is grounded in *asking open-ended, observation and application questions. Open-ended* _____ are those that typically start with '*How*,' '*What*,' '*When*,' and '*Where*,' that requires *more than just a yes or no answer*.

Observation Questions

Observation questions are more invasive in that they require thoughtful answers. The '*Serendipity* _____' is a good resource for observation and application questions, on almost every portion of Scripture in the Bible.

Observation questions ask the:

"What do I (first person) learn from this Scripture, or teaching?"
"What message in this Scripture is addressing areas of my life?"

Application Questions

_____ *questions* and answers, primarily, will **provide solutions** or on the *'How to' put things into practice*. For example:

"How can I do this?"
"What do I need to do to put this into practice?"
"Where do I start?"
"What are the steps I need to take to make this true in my life and circumstances?"

Listening Skills

For these questions to have the **transformational impact** we pray for, we also need to apply our _____ *skills to hear* what is communicated **orally and non-verbally**. The Bible teaches us the importance of listening before we speak.

> *James 1:19 Listening and Doing "19 My dear brothers, take note of this: _____ should be quick to listen, slow to speak and slow to become angry,"*

> *Proverbs 18:13 "13 He who answers before **listening**— that is his folly and his shame."*

For us to be effective in facilitating transformation in our disciples, we need to *give our full attention when our people speak.*

Here we have a few good pointers on *How to be a good listener*:

- *Do not interrupt them* when they speak.
- *Discern the underlying spirit* from which they speak.
- *Pay attention* to their *non-verbal communication*.
- *Repeat the key points* of what they are saying, so that they know that *you are listening to them*, as well as it serves to communicate that *you heard their main concerns, struggles*, or *emphasis*, and *give an opportunity* to *clarify what you are hearing*.
- *Ask questions for clarification*. It usually *encourages them to speak more, especially* when *they have a sense that you seem to get something* that they attempted to communicate.
- *Do not jump to conclusions* too hastily.
- *Do not sit in judgement* over those people who took the courage to open up and speak up. *This is an opportunity to help their transformation*, especially when you *follow their openness up* with *words of mercy and grace*, and *offer practical advice* on next steps.

Good listening will often lead your disciples to deeper _____ *and self-revelation*, which in turn could lead to a deeper and more meaningful relationship, and *a deeper relationship with the Lord*.

Remember the _____ Window!

Communication Skills

It is common knowledge that people remember only around ____% *of the what they hear* (**Verbal.**) The emphasis we place on our words (**non-verbal**), accelerates our words with another ____%, however, the way in which we posture ourselves (**para-verbal**) adds another _____% to our effective communication.

If you wish to break this down to further understand how we may use our *Verbal, Para-Verbal and Non-Verbal communication skills* to have the maximum impact when we share, we need to expand these three dimensions to many more to include *written* communication, *emotiona*l communication, and *listening* communication.

We all communicate every day, in every situation, whether we intentionally do so or not, we do. The awareness I wish to leave with you today is that *there are ways to communicate which are more effective and beneficial* for us to have a greater impact when we intend to lead people in their walk with God.

Things to consider when you communicate is:

- *Your choice* and *use of language* over that of any other person in the room.
- *The intentional use* and *meaning of the words* you choose to use when you speak.
- *The way we structure our sentences* has a determined impact.
- *The Pitch, tone and rhythm in our voice speaks volumes*, and has determined different meanings and impact.
- *The volume you use* (how *loud or soft*) can equally soften or impact a conversation.
- *The Speed with which we speak* has a determined impact on what and how we communicate.

What *is important, is that we balance these with a consistent predetermination* to, *equip by teaching things* that are both *real and observable in our lives*, as well as *ensure* that *our disciples actually learn* and *practice* these in their own lives.

We can be fool hardy to simply bring a teaching without observing whether they *"got it"* or whether they actually put it into observance. *Our calling is to ensure* that *they put into practice* what we teach. I once heard that: *"You have not taught until they have learned."*

Concluding communication skills

It is *always easier to teach, and Disciple, new Believers* than people who have been 'churched.' New Believers are like sponges in their new-found faith and open to learn all they can '*to be like Jesus.*'

My prayer is that **the Lord will use you to reach the 2/3 of the world population** who have never given their lives to the Lord. I pray that they will be like sheep and not goats. I pray that they will want to learn and that the seed of the Word will fall on good soil. I pray that you will fulfill the Call to **"teach them to obey everything I have taught you."**

Stages of forming a group

In leading and developing a group of disciples to form a cohesive body of Believers who live together in harmony and work towards a common goal and purpose, we need to also understand the various stages a group go through until they become that unified and on-purpose group.

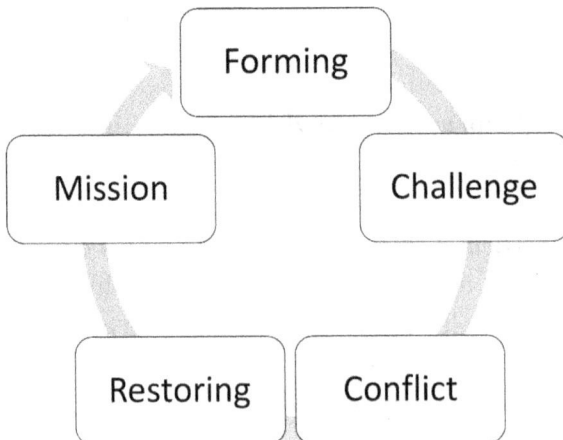

```
        Forming

Mission          Challenge

     Restoring    Conflict
```

Stages of Group Forming

Forming Stage

The first is the _____ *stage* where *we bring people together who were previously unrelated.* During this stage people find themselves *being courteous and polite*, given that it is a Christian gathering, and they do not know much about each other. Typical *level 1 and 2 communication* will be experienced as *people speak in clichés* and as *they assess each other* regarding the *factual communication that transpires.*

Challenge Stage

The second stage is where people in the group *start to* _____ *each other* with *whatever they share, stand for, or even regarding their participation*, or non-participation, in the group. *The challenge stage is a courteous stage* where *people muscle each other* to *find some kind of pecking order* in the group.

This is not really the biggest challenge in forming and leading a unified and purposeful group. *The key* is to *bring every diversion back to the purpose of the group* and to *appeal to their decision* and *commitment to follow Christ* and to grow up in Him as their Lord and Master. During this stage you will *experience level 3 kind of relationship building* happen as *people start to share and assess ideas and* _____.

During *this stage of group development* we need to keep in mind that *a.) these are sheep*, who need shepherding into their God-given life and purpose, and *b.) they are assimilating new ideas and concepts* that are for most parts *foreign to that taught in the world*, and *c.) they are doing this whilst growing and developing new relationships* within a new and often foreign relational environment. *They are challenged* and face these challenges *simultaneously* at a few different levels at the same time.

The challenge stage consists of being *relationally* challenged, *spiritually* challenged, and *culturally challenged*. They often feel *challenged personally* as it relates to their growth and assimilation of the Values and Disciplines of the Kingdom of God. They are *challenged relationally* as they sense the synergy and mutual accountability being developed in the group.

As Shepherds, this calls for our deep prayer and intercession for and on behalf of them. *Many people* can be *overwhelmed* by this *accentuated process to change and transformation.*

Some _____ and *some take* _____ as they become aware of *the challenge that is calling them* to "*conflict through*" to *a new life in Christ.*

Conflict Stage

The Conflict stage is where personalities come to a _____ *with each other.* The *tolerance level* of many people seems to be *tested beyond their spiritual maturity.* They often find themselves in *conflict with you* as the one bringing these new things into their lives.

Don't take it personal!

People often challenge you about *the things you teach* them, and *the ways of the Word* that you present to them. These, often *new concepts and values*, bring them to a place where they realise that *they need to make life-changing decisions.* They often, because of the Grace of God and the powerful work of the Holy Spirit, *repent, change and transform*, but sometimes *not before a major conflict* within *themselves* or *with others* with whom they do life with. *Expect the conflict*, but remember, it is because they are *transforming from darkness to light*, from death to life.

Restoring Stage

The Restoring stage is where things restore to the new _____. You will find that *they transition* from an *old lifestyle to a new.* You will see how *their language*, their *manners*, and their *behavior change.* You will see a new *eagerness and sincerity in their walk* with God. I always remember 2 Corinthians 7 when I see this *transformation.*

> 2 Corinthians 7:11 **See what this godly sorrow has produced in you:** *what **earnestness**, what **eagerness** to clear yourselves, what indignation, what alarm, what **longing**, what **concern**, what **readiness** to see justice done. At every point you have proved yourselves to be innocent in this matter.*

During the Restoring stage you will see the disciples *actively engage the Word, the Holy Spirit, and Christian living.* You will observe their *earnestness and eagerness.* You will observe how they *accept each other in love.* You will see how *relationships are restored.* You will observe a *humility and humanity* within those who transitioned out of the conflict stage.

The *first* _____ *of true transformation* will be their *eagerness to do something* to *make a difference.* It is these comments and conversations that will bring the group to the next stage of their forming, and that is *to become the Body of Christ* and to *fulfill their God-given purpose.*

Mission Stage

The Mission Stage is where you see these *disciples start* _____ *their faith, leading* _____ *to Christ, form their* _____ *discipleship groups,* and *committing themselves to be examples* against whom people measure their growth and development. *We have all been called for a purpose.* Fulfilling that purpose come on the back end of *a journey of forming,* being *challenged, waring through change, transforming into a committed follower of Jesus Christ,* and finally *desiring to serve Him,* and *fulfilling His Purpose* for our lives. God is calling each one of us to be on Mission with Him.

Conclusion

I pray that you will have seen these stages play out in your own life-group, and I pray that you will now be one of those gentle and wise Shepherds who will help and guide many through their transformation into pursuing Christ with all their hearts, minds and souls.

Assimilation Sheet for
The Practical Application

1. Complete the sentence. *The equipping process deals with the intentional equipping towards transitioning _____ and accountability from ourselves to those we lead and care for.*

2. Complete the sentence. *During their initial few years, the relationship is led by us being highly _____ and instructive.*

3. Complete the sentence. *The discipleship process develops from an initial _____ directive and _____ facilitation approach, to ultimately relating with _____ directive instruction and _____ facilitation.*

4. Complete the sentence. *In directive learning we _____, we _____ and we direct the course of learning and understanding.*

5. Complete the sentence. *In Facilitation we provide more emphasised _____, by asking open-ended and _____ questions.*

6. Which Equipping process is applicable when teaching through the Steps of the Discipleship Foundation Series?

- *Step One - Salvation -_____*
- _____
- *Step Two - Values and Spiritual Disciplines -_____*
- _____
- *Step Three - Developing Gifts and Skills -_____*
- _____
- *Step Four - Fruitfulness -_____*
- _____
- *Step Five - Multiplication -_____*
- _____

7. Define Open-ended questions. _____

_____

8. Define Observation Questions. Name one Good resource that you can use to help you ask good observation questions from the Bible? _____

_____

9. Define Application Questions. Give a few examples of good application questions. _____

_____
_____
_____
_____

10. What will release transformational power in our disciples when we ask these questions? _____

_____
_____

11. Outline a few ways in which we could be better listeners.

_____
_____
_____
_____
_____
_____
_____
_____
_____

12. What percentage impact does each of the following ways of communication have when we communicate?

- ____% Verbal
- ____% Non-Verbal
- ____% Para-verbal

13. Name the Five Stages of Group Forming, with a brief description of the stage, as well as the type of communication that exist in each stage.

- _____
- _____
- _____

- _____
- _____
- _____
- _____
- _____
- _____
- _____

8

CONSECRATION SESSION
SESSION EIGHT

*Acts 20:28 Keep watch over yourselves and all the flock of which the
Holy Spirit has made you overseers. Be shepherds of the church
of God, which he bought with his own blood.*

The Apostle Paul sums up His appeal to the gentile Elders in
Ephesus with a few charges.

Firstly, he exhorts them to "keep watch" over themselves.
Look after yourselves, spiritually, mentally, emotionally, and physi-
cally. Keep yourselves in step with what the Holy Spirit desires to do
in and through you. Keep watch that you keep your conversations
wholesome and seasoned, your example safeguarded, and your walk
above reproach.

*His second appeal is that they "keep watch" over all the flock of which
the Holy Spirit has made them overseers.* This is exactly what the Holy
Spirit is doing and will be doing with each one of us, He will entrust
sheep to our care and prayerful watch. We need to be careful to *"keep
watch"* over those entrusted to our care. This might start with one or
two disciples, but later it might extend to *"keeping watch"* over a
whole congregation.

Finally, He reminds them that these "sheep" has been "bought with

His own Blood," and as His Shepherds, we need to take care of His sheep.

We also have the exhortation of the Apostle Peter to his Jewish Brothers through his first pastoral letter to them.

> *1 Peter 5:2-4 Be shepherds of God's flock that is under your care, serving as overseers—not because you must, but because you are willing, as God wants you to be; not greedy for money, but eager to serve; 3 not lording it over those entrusted to you, but being examples to the flock. 4. And when the Chief Shepherd appears, you will receive the crown of glory that will never fade away.*

The Apostle Peter sums up the heart and call of the New Testament Shepherd within these few verses. His exhortation starts with a charge: "*Be Shepherds of God's flock.*"

- The first instruction is to "*be a Shepherd.*"
- The second exhortation is to "*take care*" of the sheep.
- The third is to "*serve.*" In the Kingdom of God, it's all about serving, not because we have to, but because we are "*willing.*" Our "*willingness to serve*" is seen by the extent to which we are willing to serve those whom He place under our care and oversight. Many people shy away from this kind of responsibility and serving, but here we see that it is "*as God wants you to be.*" God desires that we willingly and eagerly serve as overseers.
- The fourth observation from this portion of Scripture is the emphasis that we are actually "*entrusted*" with the care of His sheep. We need to live up to the entrustment.
- The fifth emphasis is on "*being examples to the flock.*"
- The sixth emphasis is one a few cautionary notes. This highly directive portion of Scripture covers a few "*not's,*" "*not because you must,*" "*not greedy for money,*" and "*not lording it over those entrusted to you.*"

- The final emphasis is on the reward for giving yourself to this cause and purpose. This portion ends with a wonderful promise of "*a Crown of Glory*" for those who served the Lord in this way. There might not be must glory in serving as a Shepherd in this life, but there will most certainly be a reward for those who willingly serve the Lord and His Sheep in eternity.

At one point the Apostle Paul gave a charge to his spiritual son Timothy, and with that we wish to give you a charge to take care of those whom the Lord will entrust to your care. The first portion of Chapter 4 of the First Letter to Timothy and Chapter 4 in the Second Letter to Timothy speaks amply on the stewardship and our part.

> *1 Timothy 4:11-16 Command and teach these things. Don't let anyone look down on you because you are young, but set an example for the believers in speech, in life, in love, in faith and in purity. Until I come, devote yourself to the public reading of Scripture, to preaching and to teaching. Do not neglect your gift, which was given you through a prophetic message when the body of elders laid their hands on you. Be diligent in these matters; give yourself wholly to them, so that everyone may see your progress. Watch your life and doctrine closely. Persevere in them, because if you do, you will save both yourself and your hearers.*

> *1 Timothy 6:11-13 Paul's Charge to Timothy "11 But you, man of God, flee from all this, and pursue righteousness, godliness, faith, love, endurance and gentleness. 12 Fight the good fight of the faith. Take hold of the eternal life to which you were called when you made your good confession in the presence of many witnesses. 13 In the sight of God, who gives life to everything, and of Christ Jesus, who while testifying before Pontius Pilate made the good confession, I charge you "*

2 Timothy 4:1-2 "*1 In the presence of God and of Christ Jesus, who will judge the living and the dead, and in view of his appearing and his kingdom, I give you this charge: 2 Preach the Word; be prepared in season and out of season; correct, rebuke and encourage–with great patience and careful instruction.*"

2 Timothy 4:5 But you, keep your head in all situations, endure hardship, do the work of an evangelist, discharge all the duties of your ministry.

With these words we want to charge you to go and "*Be Shepherds over God's Flock*," as willing servants of God, "*keep watch over the Sheep*" entrusted to your care. "*Be examples*" to the sheep in every aspect of your life, "*set an example for the believers in speech, in life, in love, in faith and in purity.*" May God grant you the strength to endure, the patience to persevere and the courage to preach the Word even though it might feel as if you are the only person on the planet pursuing God, His Will and His Word.

Remember, you are never alone! The Holy Spirit is with us always.

Go, and Shepherd God's People.

PART II

OTHER BOOKS BY DR. HENDRIK J VORSTER

OTHER BOOKS BY DR HENDRIK J VORSTER

Discipleship Foundations - Step One - Salvation Disciple Manual

Step One - Salvation

This Course explores the "How to" be Born Again and to establish a solid Foundation for your faith in Jesus Christ. It is based on Hebrews chapter 6 verses 1 and 2, and explores:

Repentance of dead works,
Faith in God,
Baptisms,
Laying on of hands,
Resurrection of the dead, and
Eternal Judgement

Teacher Manuals and Video Teaching material are available from our website: www.churchplantinginstitute.com

Discipleship Foundations Step Two - Values and Spiritual Disciplines Disciple Manual

Step Two - Values and Spiritual Disciplines Disciple Manual

This Course explores the "How to" develop spiritual disciplines as well as 52 Values Jesus taught. It is based on the teachings of Jesus to His Disciples, and explores:

Spiritual Disciplines

The disciplines we explore are: Reading, meditating on the Word of God, Prayer, Stewardship, Fasting, Servanthood, Simplicity, Worship, and Witnessing.

Values of the Kingdom of God

Humility, Mournfulness, meekness, Spiritual Passion, Mercifulness, Purity, Peacemaker, Patient endurance, Example, Custodian, Reconciliatory, Resoluteness, Loving, Discreetness, Forgiving, Kingdom of God Investor, God-minded, Kingdom of God prioritiser, Introspective, Persistent, Considerate, Conservative, Fruit-bearing, Practitioner, Accountability, Faithful, Childlikeness, Unity, Servanthood, Loyalty, Gratefulness, Stewardship, Obedience, Carefulness, Compassion, Caring, Confidence, Steadfastness, Contentment, Teachable, Deference, Diligence, Trustworthiness, Gentleness, Discernment, Truthfulness, Generous, Kindness, Watchfulness, Perseverance, Honouring and Submissive.

Teacher Manuals and Video Teaching material are available from our website: www.churchplantinginstitute.com

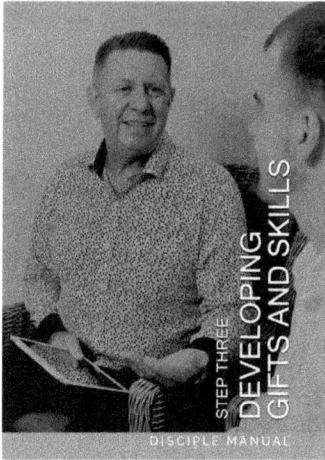

Discipleship Foundations Step Three - Developing Gifts and Skills

Step Three - Developing Gifts and Skills

This course is run through five weekend encounters. These weekend encounters have been designed to help Disciples discover their spiritual gifts, as well as learn skills to use their gifts, and to serve the Lord for the extension of His Kingdom. The Weekend Encounters are:

Gifts Discovery Weekend Encounter

We learn about Ministerial Office gifts, Service gifts, and Supernatural Spiritual Gifts. We discover our own, and then learn How we may use them to build up the local Church.

Survey of the Bible Weekend Encounter

During this weekend we do a survey of the Bible, from Genesis to Revelation. We also learn about the History of the Bible as well as How we can make most of our time in the Word.

Sharing your Faith Weekend Encounter

During this weekend we learn about the Gospel message, and How to share our faith effectively.

Overcoming Weekend Encounter

During this weekend we deal with those thistles and thorns that smother the growth and harvest of the good seed sown into our lives. We address How to overcome fear, unforgiveness, lust and the cares of the world with faith and obedience.

Shepherd Leader Weekend Encounter

During this weekend encounter we learn about being a Good Shepherd, and How to best disciple in a small group.

Teacher Manuals and Video Teaching material are available from our website: www.churchplantinginstitute.com

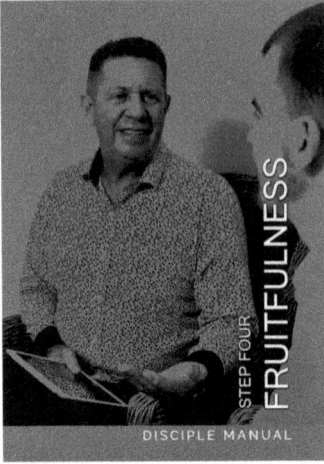

Discipleship Foundations Step Four - Fruitfulness

Step Four - Fruitfulness

We were saved to serve. This course has been designed to mobilise Believers from Learners to Practitioners. These sessions have been prepared for individual use with those who are producing fruit.

We explore:

1. Introduction.

2. Walking with purpose.

3. Build purposeful relationships. Finding Worthy Men

4. Priesthood. Praying effectively for those entrusted to you.

5. Caring compassionately.

6. Walking worthily.

7. Walking in the Spirit.

8. Practicing hospitality.

Teacher Manuals and Video Teaching material are available from our website: www.churchplantinginstitute.com

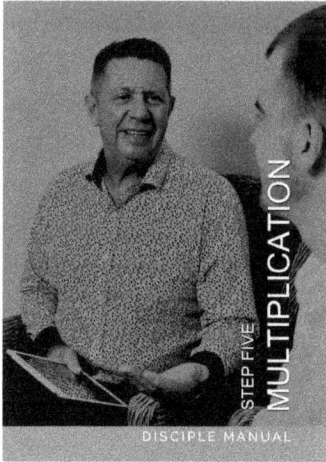

Discipleship Foundations Step Five - Multiplication

Step Five - Multiplication

This course was designed to assist fruit-producing disciples to live a life that will encourage a lifetime of fruitfulness. It will also give disciples skills and guidelines to navigate their disciples through seasons of challenge and growth. We explore:

1. Vision and dreams.

2. Set Godly Goals.

3. Character development

4. Gifts development

Impartation and Activation

5. Fruitfulness comes through constant challenge.

6. Relationships

Family, Children and Friends

7. The Power of encouragement

8. Finances

Personal and Ministry finances

9. Dealing with setbacks

- How to deal with failure?
- How to deal with betrayal?
- How to deal with rejection?
- How to deal with trials?
- How to deal with despondency?

10. Eternal rewards

Teacher Manuals and Video Teaching material are available from our website: www.churchplantinginstitute.com

VALUES
OF THE
KINGDOM
OF
GOD

Dr. Hendrik J. Vorster

Values of the Kingdom of God
By Dr. Hendrik J Vorster

Everyone desires to be known as a pleasant to be around with kind of person. This book helps you develop values towards such a godly character. This book explores 52 Values of the Kingdom of God.

Books are available from our website: www. churchplantinginstitute.com

SPIRITUAL DISCIPLINES
OF THE
KINGDOM
OF
GOD

Spiritual Disciplines of the Kingdom of God
By Dr. Hendrik J Vorster

Every Believer desires to be a Fruit-producing branch in the Vineyard of our Lord. Developing spiritual disciplines is to develop spiritual roots from which our faith can draw sap to grow strong and fruit-bearing branches. This Book explores Nine Spiritual Disciplines of the Kingdom of God.

Books are available from our website: www.churchplantinginstitute.com

Church Planting

How to plant a dynamic church

Dr. Hendrik J. Vorster
Foreword by: Dr. Yonggi Cho

Church Planting - by Dr Hendrik J Vorster

Church Planting - How to plant a dynamic, disciple-making church

By Dr Hendrik J Vorster

This is a handbook for those who wish to plant a disciple-making church. This book explores every aspect of church planting, and is widely used in over 70 Nations on 6 Continents. Here is a list of the areas that are explored:

1. The challenge to plant New Churches
2. Phases of Church Planting
3. Phase One of Church Planting - The Calling, Vision and Preparation Phase
4. The Call to Church Planting
5. Twelve Characteristics of Church Planting Leaders
6. Church Planting Terminology
7. Phase Two of Church Planting - Discipleship
8. The Process of Discipleship
9. Phase Three of Church Planting - Congregating the Discipleship Groups
10. Understanding Church Planting Finances
11. Understanding Church staff
12. Phase Four of Church Planting - Ministry development and Church Launching Phase
13. Understanding and Implementing Systems
14. Phase Five of Church Planting - Multiplication
15. Understanding the challenges in Church Planting
16. How to succeed in Church Planting
17. How to plant a House Church

Student Manuals and Video Teaching material are available from our website: www.churchplantinginstitute.com

Discipleship Foundation Series on Video

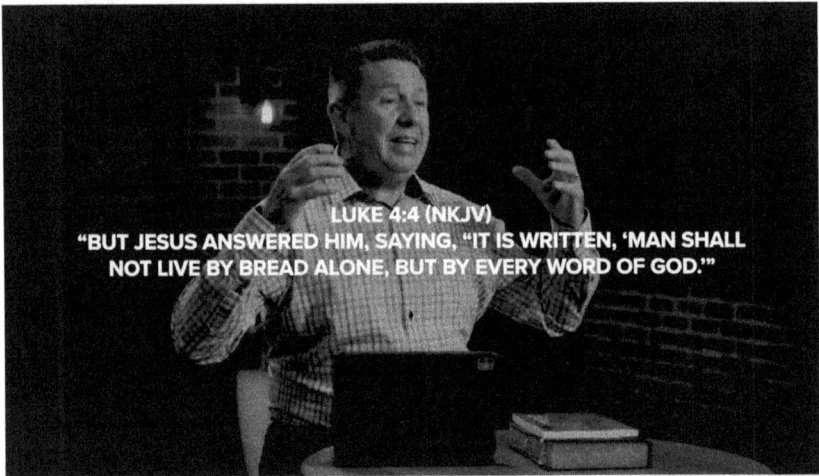

Dr. Vorster teaching via Video

185 Video Teachings are available for each of the Sessions taught throughout these Discipleship Courses.

Discipleship Foundation Series

We have Five, completely recorded, Discipleship Courses available on Video at www.discipleshipcourses.com

- **Step One - Salvation** (*This 7-week course helps the new Believer to establish, and build a solid Foundation for their faith to build on.*) This course is available, **without charge**, upon free registration.
- **Step Two - Values and Spiritual Disciplines** (*This 9-week Course helps the young Believer to put down Spiritual Roots, by establishing spiritual disciplines, and by learning the values of the Kingdom of God.*)
- **Step Three - Developing Gifts and Skills** (*This Course is usually presented during 5 Weekend Encounters, or over a 23-week period. We explore Spiritual Gifts and How to use them*

*to build up the local Church. We **explore the Bible**, and its origins, during one part to ensure we build our lives on the Handbook of the Bible. We also learn **How to share our faith.** We learn **How to deal with Strongholds** that might hold us back in fulfilling God's purpose. And finally, we learn **How to best Mentor** those whom we lead to Christ.)*

- **Step Four - Discipling Fruit-Producers** *(During this **8-week course** we learn How to teach our Disciples the principles that will develop, and maintain, fruitfulness.)*
- **Step Five - Multiplication** *(During this **11-week Course** we learn **How to Mentor our Leaders** to lead strong and healthy Fruit-producers.)*

Free registration for access to these Video resources is available at www.dicipleshipcourses.com

Church Planting Training Videos

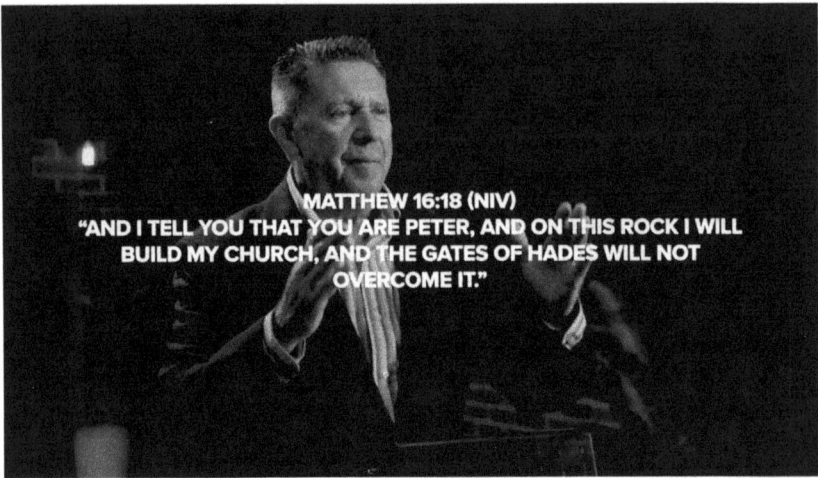

Dr. Vorster teaching via Video

42 Video Teachings are available in this **Church Planting Course.**

- Introduction to Church Planting
- Why plant New Churches?
- Phases of Church Planting Overview
- Phase 1 - Preparation Phase
- Phase 2 - Team Building Phase
- Phase 3 - Prelaunch Phase
- Phase 4 - Launch Phase
- Phase 5 - Multiplication Phase
- Church Planting Trials
- Next Steps

Free Enrolment is available at www.churchplantingcourses.com
Advanced Coaching sessions are available for those who enrolled in the Masters Training Program.

ENDNOTES